Also by the author
100% American

The
Great
Divide

How Females and Males
Really Differ

Daniel Evan Weiss

Illustrated by Steven Guarnaccia

POSEIDON PRESS

New York   London   Toronto   Sydney   Tokyo   Singapore

Poseidon Press
Simon & Schuster Building
Rockefeller Center
1230 Avenue of the Americas
New York, New York 10020

Copyright © 1991 by Daniel Evan Weiss
Illustrations Copyright © 1991 by Steven Guarnaccia

POSEIDON PRESS is a registered trademark
of Simon & Schuster.
POSEIDON PRESS colophon is a trademark
of Simon & Schuster.

Designed by Karolina Harris
Manufactured in the United States of America

1   3   5   7   9   10   8   6   4   2

Library of Congress Cataloging-in-Publication Data
Weiss, Daniel Evan.
The great divide: how females and males really differ/Daniel Evan Weiss;
illustrated by Steven Guarnaccia.
p. cm.
Includes bibliographical references.
1. Women—United States—Miscellanea—Statistics. 2. Men—United
States—Miscellanea—Statistics. 3. Sex role—United States—Miscellanea
—Statistics. 4. Sex differences (Psychology)—Miscellanea—
Statistics. I. Title.
HQ1410.W45   1991
305.3′021—dc20   90-23720
CIP
ISBN 0-671-70982-2

Acknowledgments

Kind thanks to:
Thomas Miller of the Roper Organization, Inc.; Wayne Parsons of Kane, Parsons, and Associates, Inc.; Barbara Haber of the Schlesinger Library on the History of Women in America, Radcliffe College; Jill Hodge of Louis Harris and Associates, Inc.; Maria Morales-Harper of the Bureau of the Census; Ingrid Groller of *Parents* magazine; Mary Hama of the Human Nutrition Information Service of the U.S. Department of Agriculture; Carol Weiss of the Harvard University Graduate School of Education; Joan Parks of the Metropolitan Life Insurance Company; Jeffrey Harris of R. H. Bruskin Associates Market Research; and Ann Patty.

To females—as genders go, my favorite

Contents

Preface   11

First: The Numbers   13

1.   Marriage, Divorce, and Home Life   17
2.   Crime and Drugs   41
3.   Romance and Sex   65
4.   Work and Money   89
5.   School   109
6.   Social and Political Issues   121
7.   Knowledge and Beliefs   141
8.   TV, Movies, and Books   153
9.   Sports and Leisure   169
10. Bodies and Beauty   189
11. Food   203
12. Health and Death   217
13. This and That   233

Appendix   245

Preface

It is now a generation since I began my quest to comprehend the difference between females and males. Like any youth, I always knew there was one; it just didn't much matter. And then suddenly it did. So violently and unexpectedly, in fact, that my brain proved not just unequal, but almost irrelevant, to the enterprise.

My mother assured me that all would become clear in time. It didn't. So I decided to abandon my faulty intuitions and return to the technique I used in *100% American*—I have compiled the research of hundreds of government agencies, pollsters, scientists, sociologists, psychologists, and other observers of the human condition in America, and now I let their data speak. There is a reference number at the end of each entry that keys it to its source, listed in the appendix.

If there can be a single conclusion from so vast a stock of information, mine is this—though most of the burning questions of my youth may have been answered, the magic of the Great Divide perhaps can never be. . . .

First:
The Numbers

Females and Males Here and There

Approximately 125 male fetuses are conceived for every 100 female fetuses.   252

105 baby boys are born for every 100 baby girls.   101

33% more boys than girls die in the first year of life.   252

If parents could choose the sex of their babies, 27% would have a boy. 16% would have a girl.   181

There are 100 males age 18 for each 100 females.   252

There are 68 males age 65 and older for each 100 females.   101

There are 44 males over age 85 for every 100 females.   181

For every 100 white females there are 96 males. For every 100 black females there are 88 males.   272

In 1860 there were 105 males per 100 females. In 1980 there were 95 males per 100 females   254

In 1820 the median age of females was 17; males, 17.   201

In 1970 the median age of females was 29; males, 27.   201

Females and Males Expect to Live

At birth a female is expected to live 78.3 years. A male is expected to live 71.3 years.   101

The average life expectancy for a 25-year-old female is 80. For a 25-year-old Mormon female it is 86.   194

The average life expectancy for a 25-year-old male is 74. For a 25-year-old Mormon male it is 85.   194

At age 85 a female has a life expectancy of 6.4 years. For a male it is 5.2 years.   160

68% of females
48% of males   } survive to age 75.   181

55% of females
33% of males   } survive until 80.   181

39% of females
20% of males   } survive until 85.   181

In 1900 the life expectancy for a female was 48.3 years. For a male it was 46.3 years.   201

In 1900 the life expectancy for a nonwhite female was 33.5 years. For a nonwhite male it was 32.5 years.   201

1

Marriage, Divorce, and Home Life

Females and Males Get Hitched

19% of females⎫
25% of males ⎭ age 18 and over are single.   101

61% of females⎫
66% of males ⎭ age 18 and over are married.   101

In 1890 the median age of first marriage for females was 22 years. For males it was 26.1 years.   256

In 1950 the median age of first marriage for females was 20.3 years. For males it was 22.8 years.   256

The median age of first marriage for females is 23.6 years. For males it is 25.9 years.   150

95,000 females⎫
16,000 males ⎭ age 17 or under are married.   150

22% of females⎫ age 75 and over are married and living
66% of males ⎭ with their spouse.   292

In 67% of marriages, the groom is older than the bride. In 22% of marriages, the bride is older than the groom.   101

Brides are, on average, 5.3 years younger than grooms.   101

When they remarry, wives are, on average, 3.7 years younger than their husbands.   181

22% of females remarry younger males. 61% of males remarry younger females.   181

There are 2,000 married couples in which the wife is under 25 and the husband is 75 or older.   156

There are 2,000 married couples in which the husband is 35–44 and the wife is 75 or older.   156

There are 121,000 marriages in which the husband is black and the wife white.   101

There are 56,000 marriages in which the wife is black and the husband white.   101

The record for most monogamous marriages by a female is 16. By a male it is 27.   102

39% of females ⎫ think going to a wedding means a good
20% of males ⎭ time.   286

The oldest recorded bride was 100. The oldest bridegroom was 103.   102

In 1890 there were 1,400 married 14-year-old females and 23 married 14-year-old males.   201

In 1970 there were 22,000 married 14-year-old females and 20,800 married 14-year-old males.   201

Females and Males Think about Marriage

81% of females⎱ think the good of marriage outweighs
79% of males ⎰ the bad. 270

8% of females⎱ think the bad of marriage outweighs the
5% of males ⎰ good. 270

76% of females⎱
76% of males ⎰ age 8–12 plan to get married. 162

36% of female⎱ high school seniors think one sees so few
31% of male ⎰ good or happy marriages that one questions marriage as a way of life. 313

39% of female⎱ high school seniors think that it is usually
55% of male ⎰ a good idea for a couple to live together before getting married in order to find out whether they really get along. 313

87% of female⎱ high school seniors think that it is likely
81% of male ⎰ that they will stay married to the same person for life. 313

50% of married females⎱ would marry the same person if
77% of married males ⎰ they had it to do all over again. 181

63% of females⎱ in their second marriages would marry
82% of males ⎰ the same person if they had it to do all over again. 181

Females and Males Split Up

For every 1,000 married females there are 156 divorced females. For every 1,000 married males there are 110 divorced males.   150

For every 100 unmarried males age 40–44 there are 133 unmarried females.   181

For every 100 unmarried males age 45–54 there are 247 unmarried females.   181

33% of females ⎱ who are divorced were married before
14% of males ⎰ they were 20 years old.   101

In 1890 there were 12 divorced 14-year-old females and one divorced 14-year-old male.   201

In 1970 there were 1,900 divorced 14-year-old females and 1,800 divorced 14-year-old males.   201

In the year following a divorce, the woman's standard of living falls, on average, by 73%. The man's standard of living rises by 42%.   181

52% of executive women ⎱ are single or divorced.   134
  4% of executive men ⎰

2.7% of females ⎱ age 75 and over are divorced.   292
3.3% of males ⎰

23% of divorced females ⎱ think that their marriages
40% of divorced males ⎰ might ultimately have been successful if they and their spouses had tried harder to make the marriage work.   180

Ten years after marriage, 53% of those who had cohabited before marriage had divorced. 28% of those who had never cohabited had divorced. 231

67% of females
24% of males } age 75 and over are widowed. 292

49% of females
14% of males } age 65 and over are widowed. 101

52% of females
22% of males } age 75 and over live alone. 292

In 1890 there were 17 recorded 14-year-old widows. There were no recorded 14-year-old widowers. 201

In 1970 there were 5,400 14-year-old widows. There were 2,500 14-year-old widowers. 201

Females and Males and Why They Split Up

70% of females
59% of males } cite poor communication as a cause of divorce. 191

60% of females
47% of males } cite basic unhappiness as a cause of divorce. 191

56% of females
25% of males } cite emotional abuse as a cause of divorce. 191

33% of females
29% of males } cite money problems as a cause of divorce. 191

32% of females
30% of males } cite sexual problems as a cause of divorce. 191

30% of females⎱ cite alcohol abuse by their spouses as a
6% of males ⎰ cause of divorce. 191

25% of females⎱ cite infidelity by their spouses as a cause
11% of males ⎰ of divorce. 191

4% of females⎱ cite their own infidelity as a cause of di-
6% of males ⎰ vorce. 191

22% of females⎱ cite physical abuse as a cause of divorce.
4% of males ⎰ 191

9% of females⎱
4% of males ⎰ cite children as a cause of divorce. 191

3% of females⎱ **cite women's lib as a cause of divorce.**
15% of males ⎰ 191

23% of Catholic females⎱ think it is a sin for married cou-
32% of Catholic males ⎰ ples to divorce. 124

53% of females⎱ think divorce should be more difficult to
42% of males ⎰ obtain than it is now. 324

Females and Males and the Effects of Divorce

52% of females⎱ think divorce is acceptable in cases
39% of males ⎰ where there are young children. 173

64% of divorced females⎱ with school-age children think
41% of divorced males ⎰ the children were happier
after the divorce. 180

78% of divorced females⎱ were happier after the divorce.
65% of divorced males ⎰ 180

48% of divorced females think their husbands were happier after the divorce. 40% of divorced males think that of their wives. 180

38% of females⎱ who have close friends who went
46% of males ⎰ through a divorce think the husband was
happier after the divorce. 180

55% of females⎱ who have close friends who went
45% of males ⎰ through a divorce think the wife was
happier after the divorce. 180

Females and Males Don't Get Married

39% of females
57% of males $\Big\}$ age 25 have never married.   256

16% of females
25% of males $\Big\}$ age 30–34 have never married.   256

5.3% females
4.6% of males $\Big\}$ age 65 and over have never married.   256

There are 7,000 unmarried-couple households in which the female is 65 or over and the male is under 25 years old. There are fewer than 500 unmarried-couple households in which the male is 65 or over and the female is under 25 years old.   150

Females and Males Pay Support

995,000 women ⎱ regularly pay to support people out-
5,280,000 men ⎰ side their households. 152

324,000 women ⎱ regularly pay to support children out-
4,001,000 men ⎰ side their households. 152

1,246,000 people receive financial support from a woman outside of the household. 8,668,000 receive support from a man. 152

396,000 children receive financial help from a woman outside of the household. 6,654,000 children receive support from a man. 152

Females and Males Make Babies

472,000 babies are born to mothers ⎫ under 20 years of
105,000 babies are born to fathers ⎬ age each year.   101

31,000 babies are born to mothers ⎫ 40 years old or older
174,000 babies are born to fathers ⎬ each year.   101

35% of females executives age 40 and under are mothers.
90% of male executives age 40 and under are fathers.   157

53% of teenage females ⎫ would handle an unplanned
46% of teenage males ⎬ pregnancy by getting married
and having the baby.   113

15% of teenage females ⎫ would handle an unplanned
12% of teenage males ⎬ pregnancy by having the baby
and not getting married.   113

14% of teenage females ⎫ would handle an unplanned
12% of teenage males ⎬ pregnancy by having the baby
and giving it up for adoption.
113

3% of females ⎫ think having no children is part of the
4% of males ⎬ good life.   282

14% of females ⎫ think having four or more children is
13% of males ⎬ part of the good life.   282

In choosing among marriage, children, and career, 49% of
females and 73% of males would prefer all three.   200

82% of mothers ⎫ say their sex lives suffered after they
77% of fathers ⎬ and their partners became parents.
110

44% of mothers ⎱ say they are more in love with their
55% of fathers ⎰ partners since becoming parents. 110

Females and Males Bring Up Babies

Mothers with one or more children age 5 or over spend on average 6 hours a week on child care. Fathers average 2 hours per week. 226

Mothers with one or more children under age 5 spend on average 17 hours a week on child care. Fathers average 5 hours per week. 226

24% of married females ⎱ say they and their spouses
51% of married males ⎰ take care of the children an equal amount. 200

Mothers who have only a grade-school education spend on average 6 hours a week taking care of their children. Fathers with a grade-school education spend 2 hours a week.
226

Mothers who graduated from college spend on average 12 hours a week taking care of their children. Fathers who graduated from college spend 5 hours a week.   226

81% of females
68% of males } think children are less respectful of adult authority than when they were growing up.   179

50% of females
39% of males } think permissive child-rearing is one of the most important causes of crime in our society.   175

Females and Males Do Their Chores

Combining housework and outside employment, including commuting time, wives work 71 hours per week. Husbands work 55 hours per week.   181

Females who work full time spend an average of 25 hours a week in work around the house. Males who work full time spend 13 hours.   181

59% of wives ⎫ do more than 10 hours of housework a
22% of husbands ⎭ week. 233

Wives average 2 loads of laundry per week for every person in the household. Husbands average 1 load of laundry every two months. 181

47% of females ⎫
11% of males ⎭ ironed clothing in the past week. 270

55% of females ⎫ think most males are willing to let fe-
39% of males ⎭ males get ahead, but only if females still
do all the housework at home. 200

11% of wives ⎫ think their spouses do more than a fair
46% of husbands ⎭ share of household chores. 200

27% of wives ⎫ think their spouses do less than a fair
 3% of husbands ⎭ share of household chores. 200

43% of wives think their husbands get more time to themselves than they do. 26% of husbands think they get more time to themselves than their wives do. 200

29% of females ⎫ cleaned out their closets in the past
13% of males ⎭ week. 284

61% of females ⎫ are uncomfortable unless their homes
53% of males ⎭ are neat and clean. 312

According to Working Females:

4% of wives
23% of husbands } never use the dishwasher. 229

1% of wives
27% of husbands } never use the washing machine. 229

4% of wives
20% of husbands } never use the vacuum cleaner. 229

Females and Males Rate Their Chores

Of those who do these chores at least occasionally:

41% of females
38% of males } enjoy cooking meals.

46% of females
52% of males } don't mind it.

12% of females
10% of males } dislike it. 284

6% of females
7% of males } enjoy washing dishes.

59% of females
61% of males } don't mind it.

34% of females
31% of males } dislike it. 284

5% of females
7% of males } enjoy vacuuming.

65% of females
66% of males } don't mind it.

29% of females
19% of males } dislike it.   284

3% of females
3% of males } enjoy cleaning toilets.

39% of females
44% of males } don't mind it.

56% of females
52% of males } dislike it.   284

7% of females
7% of males } enjoy ironing.

45% of females
52% of males } don't mind it.

43% of females
38% of males } dislike it.   284

Females and Males Whack Their Kids

38% of females
47% of males } think a child who is deliberately destructive deserves physical punishment, such as a spanking. 179

22% of females
32% of males } think a child who steals deserves physical punishment. 179

14% of females
10% of males } think it's never all right for parents to hit, spank, or otherwise physically discipline their children if they have misbehaved. 302

19% of females
25% of males } were often hit, spanked, or physically disciplined by their parents when they were growing up. 302

28% of girls
72% of boys } are physically punished at home. 303

**71% of females
30% of males } say they hit or spank their kids at home.** 303

62% of parents cited in child maltreatment cases are female. 38% are male. 101

Females and Males and Role Models

79% of females
85% of males } think it is desirable for a child to have a role model. 177

15% of females
24% of males } think a rock star would be an undesirable role model for a child. 177

40% of females
33% of males } think a fashion model would be an undesirable role model for a child. 177

16% of females
 5% of males } who when growing up had unfamous role models chose their mothers.

16% of females
43% of males } chose their fathers. 177

 9% of females
18% of males } who had a role model when they were growing up think the model had no effect on them one way or the other. 177

All things considered, 91% of females and 84% of males with children who have role models approve of those models. 177

15% of females
 9% of males } think a self-made millionaire businessman would be an undesirable role model for a child. 177

Females and Males and Familes

54% of mothers
41% of fathers } think their children are involved in many of the household decisions that affect them. 299

48% of mothers
36% of fathers } think their children are a lot more involved in making family decisions than they were as children. 299

35% of female
58% of male } high school seniors think a preschool child is likely to suffer if the mother works. 185

**9% of females
19% of males } age 25–29 live with their parents. 205**

21% of female
46% of male } high school seniors think it is usually better for everyone involved if the man is the achiever outside the home and the woman takes care of the home and family. 185

54% of wives
60% of husbands } say they and their spouses spend enough time together. 200

73% of wives
80% of husbands } say their spouses are also their best friends. 323

**19% of wives
36% of husbands } say that sometimes their spouses are like gods to them. 323**

Females and Males and Parents

72% of females ⎱ speak to their parents at least once a
64% of males ⎰ week. 178

51% of females ⎱ speak to their parents-in-law at least
54% of males ⎰ once a week. 178

44% of females ⎱ seek advice on important personal deci-
44% of males ⎰ sions from their parents. 178

58% of females ⎱ say their parents seek advice from them
62% of males ⎰ on important personal decisions. 178

23% of females ⎱ seek advice on important personal deci-
25% of males ⎰ sions from their parents-in-law. 178

35% of females ⎱ say their parents-in-law seek advice
43% of males ⎰ from them on important personal decisions. 178

59% of females ⎱ would ask their parents to lend them
60% of males ⎰ money. 178

39% of females ⎱ would ask their parents-in-law to lend
42% of males ⎰ them money. 178

21% of females think their husband gets along better with her parents than with his. 14% of males think their wife gets along better with his parents than with hers.   178

58% of females⎱ age 13–17 get along better with their
43% of males ⎰ mothers than their fathers.   325

24% of females⎱ age 13–17 get along better with their fa-
27% of males ⎰ thers than their mothers.   325

Females and Males Wrangle

5% of married females⎱ sometimes argue with their
9% of married males ⎰ spouses over sex.   179

4% of married females⎱ sometimes argue with their
8% of married males ⎰ spouses about the attention they pay each other.   179

15% of married females⎱ sometimes argue with their
 9% of married males ⎰ children over people they associate with.   179

53% of married people say that when couples argue over clothing expenditures, the wife usually wins. 20% say the husband usually wins.   263

40% of people say that when couples argue over how to discipline the children, the wife usually wins. 25% say the husband usually wins.   263

50% of female⎱ high school seniors have argued or had a
39% of male ⎰ fight with their parents five or more times in the last year.   245

48% of females
24% of males } think that when couples argue over which TV programs to watch, the husband usually wins. 263

24% of females
38% of males } think the wife usually wins. 263

34% of females
37% of males } have had an argument with someone in the last week. 284

60% of females
66% of males } can imagine a situation in which they would approve of a man punching an adult male stranger. 245

Females and Males at Separate Tables

24% of family households are headed by a single mother. 3% are headed by a single father. 101

55% of black family households are headed by a single mother. 3% are headed by a single father. 101

21% of children live with just their mothers. 3% live with just their fathers. 101

50% of black children live with just their mothers. 2.5% live with just their fathers. 101

13,521,000 children under age 18 live with their mothers only. 1,808,000 children under age 18 live with their fathers only. 150

2,250,000 families are headed by a mother alone who was never married. 889,000 families are headed by a father alone who was never married. 156

Family households headed by a mother alone have an average income of $12,000. Households headed by a father alone average $24,000. 150

67% of females ⎱ raising children alone are high school
74% of males ⎰ graduates. 150

67% of females ⎱ think it is unacceptable when young
54% of males ⎰ children are living with only one parent. 173

2

Crime and Drugs

Females and Males and the Law

20% of lawyers and judges are female. 80% are male.   101

39% of new lawyers are female. 61% are male.   101

7% of state and federal judges are female. 93% are male.
132

6% of law firm partners are female. 94% are male.   132

11% of tenured law faculty are female. 89% are male.   132

7% of females⎱ have been called for jury duty in the last
7% of males ⎰ year.   282

2% of females⎱
3% of males ⎰ have served on a jury in the last year.   282

Females and Males Get Ogled and Fondled

42% of females⎱ employed by the federal government are
14% of males ⎰ sexually harassed at work.   128

19% of females⎱ employed by the federal government
10% of males ⎰ who are sexually harassed are victims of
               a higher-level supervisor.   128

 2% of females⎱ employed by the federal government
10% of males ⎰ who are sexually harassed are victims of
               a subordinate.   128

76% of sexually harassed females employed by the federal government are the victims of a lone male. 60% of sexually harassed males are victims of a lone female.   128

16% of sexually harassed females employed by the federal government are the victims of two or more males. 12% of sexually harassed males are victims of two or more females.   128

3% of sexually harassed females employed by the federal government are victims of females. 22% of sexually harassed men are victims of males.   128

44% of sexually harassed females and 25% of sexually harassed males, employed by the federal government ask the person to stop.   128

52% of sexually harassed females and 42% of sexually harassed males employed by the federal government ignore the behavior or do nothing.   128

4% of sexually harassed females and 7% of sexually harassed males employed by the federal government go along with the behavior.   128

Females and Males Punish Criminals

85% of females
76% of males } think deterring the criminal from re-peating the crime is a very important purpose of punishment.   245

80% of females
65% of males } think rehabilitation is a very important purpose of punishment of criminals.
245

73% of females
69% of males } think giving a criminal what he deserves is a very important purpose of punish-ment.   245

57% of females
41% of males } think upholding morality is a very im-portant purpose of punishment of crim-inals.   245

26% of females
24% of males } think retribution is a very important purpose of punishment of criminals.
245

Females and Males Ice Each Other

3,100 white females
8,600 white males } are murdered each year.   101

1,900 black females
7,600 black males } are murdered each year.   101

63 females
167 males } were murdered in 1900.   201

12% of those arrested for murder are female. 88% are male.   101

2,500 females⎫
6,100 males ⎬ are murdered by males each year.   127

240 females⎫
1,100 males ⎬ are murdered by females each year.   127

2.3% of murder victims are the killers' husbands. 5.2% are the killers' wives.   137

9% of wives ⎫ **killed by their spouses precipitated**
60% of husbands⎬ **their own deaths by being first to use**
             physical force or to threaten the
             spouse with a weapon.   112

0.7% of murder victims are the killers' mothers. 0.9% are the killers' fathers.   137

White females have a 1 in 369 chance of being murdered. White males have a 1 in 131 chance.   181

Black females have a 1 in 104 chance of being murdered. Black males have a 1 in 21 chance.   181

Female and Males Are Busted

1,914,000 females⎫
8,882,000 males ⎬ are arrested each year.   101

21,000 females ⎫
257,000 males ⎬ were arrested in 1932.   201

350 females ⎫
28,000 males⎬ are arrested for rape each year.   137

9,400 females⎱
102,000 males⎰ are arrested for robbery each year.   137

54,000 females⎱ are arrested for prostitution and com-
25,000 males ⎰ mercialized sex each year.   137

132,000 females⎱ are arrested for drug abuse violations
720,000 males ⎰ each year.   137

13% of those arrested for aggravated assault are female.
87% are male.   101

14% of those arrested for arson are female. 86% are male.
101

34% of those arrested for forgery and counterfeiting are
female. 66% are male.   101

38% of those arrested for embezzlement are female. 62%
are male.   101

43% of those arrested for fraud are female. 57% are male
101

57% of those arrested for running away are female. 43%
are male.   101

Females and Males Fight Crime

56% of females⎱ keep their car windows rolled up when
41% of males ⎰ they would rather have them down, because they fear crime.   175

28% of females⎱ dress more conservatively than they
17% of males ⎰ would like because they fear crime.   175

52% of females ⎱ avoid talking to strangers in public
29% of males ⎰ places. 175

91% of females ⎱ regularly lock the doors of their homes.
84% of males ⎰ 245

62% of females ⎱ are afraid to walk at night within a mile
26% of males ⎰ of their residences. 181

Female and Male Students Run Amok

5% of female ⎱ high school seniors have been threatened
12% of male ⎰ by someone with a weapon while in
school in the last year. 245

3% of female ⎱ **high school seniors have hurt someone**
29% of male ⎰ **badly enough to need bandages or a**
doctor in the last year. 245

4% of female ⎫
9% of male ⎭ high school seniors have stolen something worth over $50 in the last year. 245

20% of female ⎫
29% of male ⎭ high school seniors have gone into a house or building when they weren't supposed to be there in the last year. 245

8% of female ⎫
19% of male ⎭ high school seniors have damaged school property on purpose in the last year. 245

87% of female ⎫
71% of male ⎭ high school seniors worry about crime and violence. 245

Females and Males Are Victims

For each thousand, 40 females and 81 males age 16–19 are victims of violent crime each year. 245

For each thousand, 17 females and 23 males age 35–49 are victims of violent crime each year. 245

77% of violent crimes committed by a relative of the victim are committed against females. 23% are committed against males. 245

30% of violent crimes committed by a stranger to the victim are committed against females. 70% are committed against males. 245

21% of females
54% of males $\Big\}$ have been hit by someone. 245

73% of females
83% of males $\Big\}$ will be victims of attempted violent crimes during their lives. 245

36% of females
48% of males $\Big\}$ will be victims of completed violent crimes during their lives. 245

22% of females
37% of males $\Big\}$ will be robbed in their lifetimes. 245

99% of females
99% of males $\Big\}$ will be victims of theft in their lifetimes. 245

Females and Males and Child Abuse

The wives of 6% of male incest offenders are arrested with them. 305

10% of female | victims of child abuse suffer anal contact.
33% of male ∫ 305

19% of female | victims of child abuse have oral sex per-
41% of male ∫ formed on them. 305

17% of female | victims of child abuse perform oral sex.
29% of male ∫ 305

54% of female |
43% of male ∫ victims of child abuse are fondled. 305

7% of female |
8% of male ∫ victims of child abuse fondle. 305

15–30% of women | were sexually victimized as chil-
5–10% of men ∫ **dren.** 112

Females and Males and Guns

14% of females |
47% of males ∫ own a gun. 245

43% of females |
51% of males ∫ have a gun in the home. 245

23% of females ⎱ think having a gun in the home makes it
34% of males ⎰ a safer place. 245

43% of females ⎱ think having a gun in the home makes it
26% of males ⎰ a more dangerous place. 245

51% of females ⎱ favor laws that would make handguns
37% of males ⎰ illegal. 175

84% of females ⎱ favor a federal law requiring that all
71% of males ⎰ handguns be registered by federal au-
               thorities. 237

38% of females ⎱ think making handguns illegal would go
24% of males ⎰ a long way toward reducing crime. 175

63% of females ⎱ **think people should have the right to**
74% of males ⎰ **shoot someone who breaks into their**
               homes, even if they don't know
               whether the person is armed. 245

Females and Males Hang Them High

75% of females }
83% of males } favor the death penalty for persons con- victed of murder.   119

60% of females }
66% of males } favor the death penalty for persons con- victed of attempting to assassinate the president.   119

48% of females }
55% of males } favor the death penalty for persons con- victed of rape.   119

42% of females }
58% of males } favor the death penalty for persons con- victed of hijacking an airplane.   119

35% of females }
50% of males } favor the death penalty for spying for a foreign nation during peacetime.   119

37% of females }
52% of males } **think it is right to execute people who committed murder when they were younger than 18.**   298

19% of females }
24% of males } think that mentally retarded people who commit murder should be executed. 298

56% of females }
67% of males } feel that the death penalty acts as a de- terrent to murder.   245

71% of females }
79% of males } who favor the death penalty for murder would still favor the death penalty even if convicted murders were sent to jail for life without any chance of being let out. 245

1% of prisoners on death row are female. 99% are male. 245

Females and Males Go to the Jug

There are 29,000 female prisoners and 553,000 male prisoners in state and federal prisons. 101

20 females
423 males } for every 100,000 are in prison. 245

6 females
149 males } for every 100,000 were in prison in 1925. 245

State prisons housing females average 65 square feet per inmate. Prisons housing males average 57 square feet per inmate. 245

State prisons housing females confine their inmates to their unit 9.9 hours per day. Prisons housing males confine inmates 11.4 hours per day. 245

3% of females
20% of males } have spent a night in jail. 181

There are 6,700 female and 61,000 male correctional offi-cers. 245

There are 6,800 females and 42,500 males held in public juvenile facilities. 245

Females and Males Are Sprung

Female prisoners convicted of murder are released from state prison after serving an average of 58 months. Males serve 88 months. 245

Female prisoners convicted of kidnapping are released from state prison after serving an average of 32 months. Males serve 39 months. 245

Female prisoners convicted of robbery are released from state prison after serving an average of 24 months. Males serve 36 months. 245

Female prisoners convicted of burglary are released from state prison after serving an average of 15 months. Males serve 21 months. 245

Female prisoners convicted of motor vehicle theft are re-leased from state prison after serving an average of 15 months. Males serve 16 months. 245

Female prisoners convicted of drug trafficking are released from state prison after serving an average of 15 months. Males serve 18 months. 245

52% of females } **paroled from prison between the ages**
70% of males } **of 17 and 22 are rearrested within six years.** 245

81% of females
81% of males } favor harsher prison sentences.   281

Females and Males and Cops

11% of police and detectives are female. 89% are male.
101

2% of law enforcement officers killed in the line of duty
are female. 98% are male.   245

4% of people who kill law enforcement officers are female.
96% are male.   245

18% of females
17% of males } think police brutality is a very serious
threat to ordinary citizens.   281

13% of female
30% of male } high school seniors have gotten into trou-
ble with the police in the last year.   245

Females and Males Light Up

24% of females
30% of males } smoke.   181

48% of female
33% of male } smokers smoke less than a pack a day.
119

13% of female ⎱ smokers smoke more than a pack a day.
25% of male ⎰ 119

70% of females ⎱ have smoked cigarettes. 197
81% of males ⎰

4% of females ⎱ have used smokeless tobacco. 197
27% of males ⎰

3% of females ⎱ gave up smoking last year. 282
5% of males ⎰

Females and Males Hit the Sauce

14% of females ⎱ drink alcohol at least once a week. 197
35% of males ⎰

81% of females ⎱ have drunk alcohol. 197
90% of males ⎰

87% of females ⎱ living in the northeastern states have
90% of males ⎰ drunk alcohol. 197

76% of females ⎱ living in the southern states have drunk
87% of males ⎰ alcohol. 197

92% of female ⎫ high school seniors have drunk alcohol.
92% of male ⎭ 198

41% of females ⎫
48% of males   ⎭ age 12–17 have drunk alcohol. 197

36% of females ⎫
24% of males   ⎭ do not drink. 181

20% of female drinkers ⎫ occasionally consume five or
30% of male drinkers   ⎭ more drinks a sitting. 181

19% of female ⎫ drinkers say they sometimes drink too
38% of male   ⎭ much. 123

29% of females ⎫ perceive that they have an alcohol-
19% of males   ⎭ related family problem. 123

Females consume 20% of the beer that is drunk. Males consume 80%.   181

41% of females ⎫ think the beer industry gives good or ex-
54% of males   ⎭ cellent value for the dollar.   268

8% of females ⎫ have drunk liquor in the past week.   263
16% of males ⎭

2% of females ⎫ gave up drinking in the past year.   282
3% of males   ⎭

13% of females ⎫ oppose a national law that would raise
22% of males   ⎭ the legal drinking age in all states to 21.
245

30% of females ⎫ **do not think alcoholic beverages**
22% of males   ⎭ **should be available to any adult who**
wants them.   178

Females and Males Go Bottoms Up

In a U.S. government study of 38,000 people over a three-day period, the greatest recorded consumption:

In a day a female consumed 12 beers. A male consumed 42 beers.   213

At a sitting a female consumed 7 beers. A male consumed 24 beers.   213

In a day a female consumed 32 ounces of distilled liquor. A male consumed 44 ounces.   213

At a sitting a female consumed 32 ounces of distilled liquor. A male consumed 32 ounces.   213

Females and Males Drink and Drive

14% of females
30% of males } sometimes drive after drinking. 246

15% of female drivers } **in fatal motor vehicle accidents**
28% of male drivers } **were drunk.** 289

150,000 females
1,140,000 males } are arrested for driving under the influence each year. 137

39% of females
61% of males } in 11th or 12th grade have driven after having a drink. 255

66% of female
68% of male } students have gone for a ride with a driver who has been drinking. 255

11% of female
16% of male } high school seniors have received a traffic ticket or warning while driving under the influence of alcohol in the last year. 245

28% of females
30% of males } have been a designated driver for people who were drinking. 271

15% of females
26% of males } have been driven home by a designated driver. 271

Females and Males Get High

33% of females
40% of males } have used an illicit drug. 197

26% of females
24% of males } age 12–17 have used an illicit drug. 197

12% of females ⎱ have used an illicit drug in the past year.
16% of males ⎰ 197

30% of females ⎱ living in the north central states have
44% of males ⎰ used an illicit drug. 197

43% of females ⎱ living in the western states have used an
44% of males ⎰ illicit drug. 197

4% of females ⎱
8% of males ⎰ have used inhalants. 197

6% of females ⎱
9% of males ⎰ have used hallucinogens. 197

6% of females ⎱ say they have used more prescription
10% of males ⎰ drugs, such as Valium and amphetamines, than they should have. 178

3% of females ⎱
5% of males ⎰ have used sedatives. 197

3% of females ⎱
4% of males ⎰ have used PCP. 197

0.6% of females (659,000) ⎱ have used heroin. 197
1.3% of males (1,248,000) ⎰

**have used a needle to inject
0.7% of females (689,000)** ⎱ **themselves with cocaine,
1.9% of males (1,821,000)** ⎰ **heroin, or amphetamines.**
197

37% of female ⎱ high school seniors have used stay-awake
38% of male ⎰ pills. 198

34% of females
46% of males } would handle the matter themselves if they found out their 16-year-old was using drugs.   175

25% of females
34% of males } think that more than half of adults who use illegal drugs are otherwise law-abiding citizens.   245

83% of females
80% of males } would be willing to pay higher taxes to have much stricter prosecution and punishment of drug sellers.   263

73% of females
63% of males } would be willing to pay higher taxes to have much stricter prosecution and punishment of drug users.   263

45% of females
50% of males } favor the death penalty for major drug dealers.   285

**27% of females
35% of males } favor legalizing the sale of some drugs to make dealing drugs less profitable and reduce crime associated with drug use.   285**

Females and Males Roll Reefers

30% of females
37% of males } have used marijuana.   197

2% of females
5% of males } use marijuana at least once a week.   197

56% of females
68% of males } age 26–34 have used marijuana.   197

18% of females
17% of males } age 12–17 have used marijuana.   197

31% of white females
36% of white males } have used marijuana.   197

27% of black females
41% of black males } have used marijuana.   197

**30% of females
41% of males** } **think possession of small amounts of marijuana should not be treated as a criminal offense.**   245

39% of female
41% of male } high school seniors think people age 18 or older should be allowed to smoke marijuana in private.   313

10% of female
17% of male } high school seniors think people age 18 or older should be allowed to smoke marijuana in public places.   313

44% of females
28% of males } are not very concerned their children will use marijuana.   178

Females and Males Take It up the Nose

9% of females
13% of males } have used cocaine.   197

21% of females
32% of males } age 26–34 have used cocaine.   197

0.2% of females (196,000)⎤ use cocaine at least once a
0.7% of males (666,000) ⎦ week. 197

3% of female⎤ high school seniors have used crack. 198
6% of male ⎦

49% of females⎤ are not very concerned their children
32% of males ⎦ will use cocaine or crack. 178

Females and Males and Sniffing for Drugs

89% of females⎤ think there should be mandatory peri-
88% of males ⎦ odic drug testing of all people who operate public transportation, such as
airplanes, buses, and trains. 285

85% of females⎤ think there should be mandatory peri-
84% of males ⎦ odic drug testing of all police officers.
285

77% of females⎤ think there should be mandatory peri-
73% of males ⎦ odic drug testing of all professional athletes. 285

71% of females⎤ think there should be mandatory peri-
68% of males ⎦ odic drug testing of all government employees. 285

71% of females⎤ think there should be mandatory peri-
67% of males ⎦ odic drug testing of all schoolteachers.
285

61% of females ⎫
57% of males ⎭ think there should be mandatory periodic drug testing of prospective employees by companies considering them. 285

55% of females ⎫
48% of males ⎭ think there should be mandatory periodic drug testing of all current employees by their companies. 285

51% of females ⎫
44% of males ⎭ think there should be mandatory periodic drug testing of all students age 12 and over in public schools. 285

33% of females ⎫
27% of males ⎭ **think there should be mandatory periodic drug testing of all adult Americans.** 285

3

Romance and Sex

Female and Male Teenagers Warm to Each Other

81% of teenage females
52% of teenage males } would date someone who isn't much to look at but has personality. 113

48% of teenage females
33% of teenage males } think kindness is a reason for dating someone. 113

34% of teenage females
17% of teenage males } think manners are a reason for dating someone. 113

24% of teenage females
46% of teenage males } think sex appeal is a reason for dating someone. 113

**16% of teenage females
50% of teenage males** } **think figure or physique is a reason for dating someone.**
113

Females and Males Warm to Each Other

55% of females find a male's face the most attractive part of his body. 27% of males think that of a female's face.   181

8% of females can find a male attractive only if he has a muscular physique. 23% of males think that of a female's good figure.   172

58% of females can find a male attractive only if he is intelligent. 51% of males think that of a female.   172

3% of females can find a male attractive only if he has power and influence. 6% of males think that of a female.   172

50% of females can find a male attractive only if he is widely respected by those who know him. 37% of males think that of a female.   172

38% of females can find a male attractive only if he has religious beliefs similar to hers. 28% of males think that of a female.   172

20% of people think that having a lot of money adds to a female's sex appeal. 21% think it adds to a man's.   148

56% of females **think there is such a thing as love at**
67% of males **first sight.**   172

Females and Males on Valentine's Day

4% of females think that Mikhail Gorbachev would be a perfect companion on Valentine's Day. 7% of males think the same of Margaret Thatcher.   172

7% of females think Donald Trump would be a perfect companion on Valentine's Day. 9% of males think the same of Jackie Kennedy Onassis.   172

7% of females think Ted Koppel would be a perfect companion on Valentine's Day. 10% of males think the same of Barbara Walters.   172

Females and Males Learn about Sex

33% of females ⎱ were first told about sex by their moth-
 8% of males ⎰ ers.   250

 1% of females ⎱ were first told about sex by their fathers.
10% of males ⎰ 250

68% of mothers ⎱ of children age 8–17 feel very comfort-
48% of fathers ⎰ able talking with them about sex.   248

28% of female ⎱ college students from intact middle-class
23% of male ⎰ families have had a sexual experience with a relative.   112

 8% of females ⎱ were first told about sex by a sexual
12% of males ⎰ partner.   250

34% of females
24% of males
} think that a sex education program in schools should teach that sex should be saved for marriage. 180

20% of females
21% of males
} think sex education programs in the public schools encourage sexual activity. 180

70% of females
63% of males
} age 8–17 who have sex education classes think they're good. 244

35% of female
45% of male
} teenagers have had no sex education. 249

Females and Males and Teen Sex

37% of teenage females
58% of teenage males
} approve of premarital sex. 113

8% of teenage females
25% of teenage males
} think it's all right to be sexually involved with more than one person at a time. 113

40% of teenage females
21% of teenage males
} think it's up to the boy to start making out. 113

**45% of teenage females
22% of teenage males
} have given in to pressure to have sex.** 113

4% of teenage females would have sex to keep their boyfriends interested in the relationship. 12% of teenage males would do so to keep their girlfriends. 113

Females and Males Pay for Dates

33% of females
47% of males } think that when two young adults go out on a date, the male should pay. 182

45% of females
38% of males } think that when two young adults go out on a date, the one who asked for the date should pay. 182

17% of females
11% of males } think that when two young adults go out on a date, they should split the tab. 182

Females and Males and Romance

30% of females 8–12 have a special boyfriend. 36% of males age 8–12 have a special girlfriend. 163

27% of females
19% of males } in a marriage or romance think their partner is less romantic than desired. 174

32% of females
24% of males } think diamonds are the most romantic gift a man can give a woman. 174

**74% of females
71% of males** } **think cooking him a dinner is the most romantic gift a woman can give a man.** 174

69% of females
52% of males } strongly believe that our society places too much emphasis on sex and not enough on romance. 174

When they are with men the same age as they are, 47% of affluent women age 40–65 feel younger than the men. 11% feel older than the men.   251

21% of females ⎱ think they are more romantic than the
27% of males ⎰ average person.   174

The heart of the average woman weighs 2 ounces less than that of the average man (see p. 191).   320

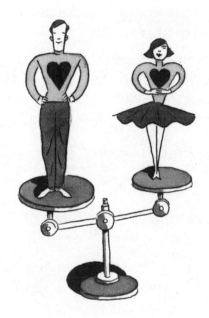

Males Subdue Females

12% of females ⎱ in high school indicate that it is accept-
39% of males   ⎰ able for a boy to force sex on a girl if he spends a lot of money on her.   189

18% of females ⎱ in high school indicate that it is accept-
39% of males   ⎰ able for a boy to force sex if the girl is stoned or drunk.   189

17% of female ⎱
2% of male ⎰ teenagers think many teenagers don't wait to have sexual intercourse until they are older because boys pressure girls into it. 249

10% of sexually active female college students and 34% of sexually active male college students have told a lie in order to have sex. 321

60% of sexually active female college students and 47% of sexually active male college students say they have been lied to for purposes of sex. 321

Females and Males and Romance at Home

37% of females ⎱
52% of males ⎰ always kiss their spouses good night. 311

26% of females ⎱
21% of males ⎰ rarely or never kiss their spouses good night. 311

In 40% of households the female usually apologizes first. In 60% the male does. 311

51% of females ⎱
55% of males ⎰ think the women's movement has made things harder for males at home. 200

Females and Males and the Fall from Grace

3% of females⎱ have had sexual intercourse by age 14.
10% of males ⎰ 211

 5% of black females⎱ have had sexual intercourse by
30% of black males ⎰ age 14. 211

 8% of females⎱ have had sexual intercourse by age 15.
17% of males ⎰ 211

18% of females⎱ have had sexual intercourse by age 16.
29% of males ⎰ 211

33% of females⎱ have had sexual intercourse by age 17.
48% of males ⎰ 211

46% of black females⎱ have had sexual intercourse by
79% of black males ⎰ age 17. 211

51% of females⎱ have had sexual intercourse by age 18.
65% of males ⎰ 211

68% of females⎱ have had sexual intercourse by age 19.
78% of males ⎰ 211

 9% of females⎱ were engaged to their first sexual part-
0.6% of males ⎰ ners. 181

55% of females⎱ were going steady with their first sexual
37% of males ⎰ partners. 181

 7% of females⎱ were friends with their first sexual part-
34% of males ⎰ ners. 181

4% of females⎱ just recently met their first sexual part-
9% of males ⎰ ners. 181

17% of females
25% of males } planned their first intercourse.   181

40% of females
60% of males } tell somebody within a month about their first coital experiences.   304

22% of females
over 50% of males } **tell 5 or more friends about their first coital experiences.**   304

40% of females
67% of males } say their parents knew about their first coital experiences.   304

59% of females
14% of males } **did not enjoy the first time they made love.**   311

16% of males
30% of females over 35
51% of females under 35 } regret having premarital sex.
317

Females and Males and Drugs and the Fall from Grace

12% of female
19% of male } 14-year-old virgins who do not use marijuana or alcohol will begin using at least one within the next year. 211

25% of females
27% of males } who have first intercourse at age 14 and who do not use marijuana or alcohol will begin using at least one within the next year. 211

20% of female
28% of male } 16-year-old virgins who do not use marijuana or alcohol will begin using at least one within the next year. 211

39% of females
43% of males } who have first intercourse at age 16 and who do not use marijuana or alcohol will begin using at least one within the next year. 211

4% of female
7% of male } 14-year-old virgins who do not use drugs or alcohol have intercourse within the next year. 211

23% of female
21% of male } 14-year-old virgins who use marijuana and alcohol have intercourse within the next year. 211

15% of female
22% of male } 16-year-old virgins who do not use drugs or alcohol have intercourse within the next year. 211

30% of female
46% of male } 16-year-old virgins who use marijuana and alcohol have intercourse within the next year. 211

26% of female
29% of male } 18-year-old virgins who do not use drugs or alcohol have intercourse within the next year. 211

53% of female
47% of male } 18-year-old virgins who use marijuana and alcohol have intercourse within the next year. 211

Females and Males and Sex

83% of females
97% of males } masturbate. 181

32% of Catholic females
37% of Catholic males } think it is a sin to masturbate. 124

91% of females
79% of males } have performed heterosexual oral sex. 181

43% of females
60% of males } have had heterosexual anal sex. 181

12% of females
8% of males } think advances in the exploration of space have gone too far. 264

5% of females
5% of males } have had sexual contact with animals. 181

**95% of lesbians
71% of gay men
80% of heterosexuals** } **kiss every time they have sex.** 233

12% of lesbians
17% of gay men } have oral sex every time they have sex. 233

6% of heterosexuals have cunnilingus and 5% have fellatio every time they have sex. 233

59% of wives ⎱ say their spouses are skilled lovers.
48% of husbands ⎰ 323

26% of females ⎱ say they enjoy sex more than money.
47% of males ⎰ 134

31% of females ⎱ think sexual relations before marriage
41% of males ⎰ are always or almost always wrong. 324

48% of Catholic females ⎱ think it is a sin for unmarried
42% of Catholic males ⎰ people to have sexual relations.
56% of Protestants 124

34% of females ⎱ think sexual relations before marriage
46% of males ⎰ are not wrong at all. 324

There are 20 clinically diagnosed male sexual masochists for every female. 138

Almost all clinically diagnosed sexual fetishists, pedophiles, sexual sadists, transvestite fetishists, and sexual voyeurs are male. 138

Females and Males and the Frequency of Sex

45% of married couples ⎱
61% of cohabitating couples ⎰ who have been together up
33% of lesbians to 2 years have sex at least
67% of gay men three times a week. 233

18% of married couples ⎱ together for 10 years or more
 1% of lesbians ⎰ have sex at least 3 times a
11% of gay men week. 233

15% of married couples ⎤ together for 10 years or more
47% of lesbians   ⎬ have sex once a month or less.
33% of gay men   ⎦ 233

Females and Males Listen at Their Parents' Doors

31% of daughters ⎤ think their mothers masturbate.   224
49% of sons   ⎦

62% of mothers masturbate.   224

63% of daughters ⎤ think their mothers engaged in pre-
69% of sons   ⎦ marital petting.   224

99% of mothers engaged in premarital petting.   224

10% of daughters ⎤ think their mothers engaged in pre-
22% of sons   ⎦ marital sex.   224

50% of mothers engaged in premarital sex.   224

2% of daughters ⎤ think their mothers engage in extra-
2% of sons   ⎦ marital sex.   224

26% of mothers engage in extramarital sex.   224

25% of daughters ⎤ think their mothers engage in oral-
30% of sons   ⎦ genital sex.   224

49% of mothers engage in oral-genital sex.   224

62% of daughters ⎤ think their fathers masturbate.   224
73% of sons   ⎦

93% of fathers masturbate.   224

80% of daughters ⎫ think their fathers engaged in premar-
81% of sons ⎭ ital petting. 224

89% of fathers engaged in premarital petting. 224

33% of daughters ⎫ think their fathers engaged in premar-
45% of sons ⎭ ital sex. 224

92% of fathers engaged in premarital sex. 224

 7% of daughters ⎫ think their fathers engage in extra-
12% of sons ⎭ marital sex. 224

50% of fathers engage in extramarital sex. 224

29% of daughters ⎫ think their fathers engage in oral-gen-
34% of sons ⎭ ital sex. 224

59% of fathers engage in oral-genital sex. 224

And what the parents think:

37% of females ⎫ with children age 18 or under have al-
34% of males ⎭ lowed the children to see a movie they
thought was too sexually explicit. 180

 5% of females ⎫ with children age 18 or under have al-
12% of males ⎭ lowed the children to look at magazines
they thought were too sexually explicit.
180

46% of females ⎫ think their sex lives have gotten better
40% of males ⎭ since their children were born. 180

Females and Males Initiate, and Refuse, Sex

12% of wives } are more likely to initiate sex than
51% of husbands } their spouses are. 233

15% of female cohabitors } are more likely to initiate sex
39% of male cohabitors } than their partners are. 233

53% of wives } **are more likely to refuse sex than**
13% of husbands } **their spouses are.** 233

43% of female cohabitors } are more likely to refuse sex
22% of male cohabitors } than their partners are. 233

78% of females } have had headaches in the last year. 168
68% of males }

Females and Males and Being True

84% of wives } are possessive of their spouses. 233
79% of husbands }

74% of lesbians } are possessive of their partners. 233
35% of gay men }

84% of wives } think it is important that they be mo-
75% of husbands } nogamous. 233

21% of wives } have been unfaithful. 233
26% of husbands }

3% of wives } who have been unfaithful have had
7% of husbands } more than 20 lovers. 233

71% of lesbians⎱ think it is important that they be mono-
36% of gay men⎰ gamous. 233

28% of lesbians⎱
82% of gay men⎰ have been unfaithful. 233

79% of partners of unfaithful lesbians and 88% of partners
of unfaithful gay men are aware of the infidelity. 233

 1% of lesbians⎱ who have been unfaithful have had
43% of gay men⎰ more than 20 lovers. 233

64% of the wives ⎱ **of an unfaithful spouse are**
28% of the husbands⎰ **aware of the infidelity.** 233

37% of wives⎱
52% of husbands⎰ approve of sex without love. 233

67% of female cohabitors⎱ approve of sex without love.
72% of male cohabitors ⎰ 233

57% of lesbians
79% of gay men } approve of sex without love.   233

Women's extramarital affairs last, on average, 21 months. Men's last 29 months.   181

Females and Males Think about Sex

4% of females
9% of males } frequently have sexual fantasies.   286

44% of females
27% of males } almost never have sexual fantasies.   286

70%–75% of females
nearly all males } report dreaming about sex at some time in their lives.   304

**40% of females
80% of males** } **report having sex dreams that result in orgasm.**   304

Females and Males and Oral Sex

In premarital foreplay, 22% of females report receiving much cunnilingus. 5% of males report providing much.   308

In marital foreplay, 20% of females report receiving much cunnilingus. 15% of males report providing much.   308

In premarital foreplay, 23% of females report providing much fellatio. 9% of males report receiving much.   308

In marital foreplay, 17% of females report providing much fellatio. 12% of males report receiving much.   308

59% of females
50% of males } who have had coitus and have been in love once have performed oral sex.   308

52% of females
63% of males } who have had coitus and have been in love at least twice have performed oral sex.   308

31% of females
36% of males } ate salty snacks in the last 24 hours.   271

Females and Males Don't Have Oral Sex

Why people who have had sexual intercourse but do not engage in oral-genital sex do not:

57% of females
24% of males } are too shy.   308

37% of females
46% of males } don't want to.   308

32% of females
 9% of males } fear their partners would lose control.   308

30% of females
22% of males } think it's immoral.   308

30% of females
49% of males } think their partners don't want to.   308

26% of females
20% of males } fear loss of reputation.   308

21% of females
 8% of males } feel they would lose control.   308

13% of females ⎱
7% of males ⎰ think their parents would disapprove. 208

4% of females ⎱
26% of males ⎰ fear VD. 308

Females and Males and Sex over 80

Among healthy, upper middle-class whites, age 80–102:

30% of females ⎱
63% of males ⎰ have sexual intercourse. 306

10% of females ⎱
29% of males ⎰ have sexual intercourse often. 306

71% of females ⎱
88% of males ⎰ have fantasized in the past year about being close, affectionate, or intimate with members of the opposite sex. 306

40% of females ⎱
72% of males ⎰ masturbate. 306

14% of females are married; 25% have regular sex partners. 29% of males are married; 53% have regular sex partners. 306

Females and Males and Birth Control

49% of females ⎫ used contraceptives the first time they
44% of males   ⎭ had sex. 181

34% of female ⎫ teenagers who have intercourse use birth
33% of male   ⎭ control every time. 249

21% of female ⎫ teenagers who have intercourse never
30% of male   ⎭ use birth control. 249

27% of female ⎫ high school seniors get a real kick out of
45% of male   ⎭ doing things that are a little dangerous.
              313

38% of sexually active teenage females and 10% of sexually active teenage males usually rely on the birth-control pill for contraception. 249

14% of Catholic females ⎫ think it is a sin for married couples to use artificial methods of
23% of Catholic males   ⎭ birth control. 124

Females and Males and Condoms

25% of sexually active teenage females and 47% of sexually active teenage males usually use condoms for contraception. 249

Male prostitutes use condoms 85–90% of the time when they are with male clients, 70–80% of the time with male lovers, 30–50% of the time with females. 203

73% of females ⎱ think the good of condoms out-
77% of males ⎰ weighs the bad. 270

12% of Catholic females ⎱ think it is sinful to use con-
18% of Catholic males ⎰ doms as a protection against AIDS.

Females and Males Would Rather Be Males and Females

90% of female-to-male transsexuals and 61% of male-to-female transsexuals are sexually satisfied. 307

70% of female-to-male transsexuals and 43% of male-to-female transsexuals retain close contact with their families. 307

57% of female-to-male transsexuals and 27% of male-to-female transsexuals form lasting romantic partnerships. 307

100% of female-to-male transsexuals and 60% of male-to-female transsexuals inform their partners about their transsexualism.

5% of female-to-male transsexuals and 21% of male-to-female transsexuals have made a suicide attempt.   307

100% of sexual partners of female-to-male transsexuals are female. 60% of sexual partners of male-to-female transsexuals are male.   307

Females and Females and Males and Males

64% of female ⎫ homosexuals have no regret about their
49% of male   ⎭ homosexuality.   188

38% of female ⎫ homosexuals have considered discontin-
29% of male   ⎭ uing homosexual activity.   188

46% of female ⎫ homosexuals say their fathers don't sus-
53% of male   ⎭ pect their homosexuality.   188

32% of female ⎫ homosexuals say their mothers don't sus-
38% of male   ⎭ pect their homosexuality.   188

16% of female ⎫ homosexuals say their heterosexual
21% of male   ⎬ friends don't suspect their homosexual-
              ⎭ ity.   188

33% of female ⎫ homosexuals never reach orgasm in het-
 8% of male   ⎭ erosexual sex.   188

55% of female ⎫ **homosexuals have heterosexual sex**
33% of male   ⎭ **dreams.**   188

45% of female ⎫ homosexuals are exclusively homosex-
55% of male   ⎭ ual.   188

38% of female ⎫ homosexuals are concerned they are not
52% of male   ⎭ sexually adequate.   188

3% of female ⎫ homosexuals spend an hour or less with
21% of male ⎭ a person they pick up while cruising.   188

24% of female ⎫ homosexuals will spend all weekend with
2% of male ⎭ a person they pick up while cruising.   188

81% of female ⎫ homosexuals had some affection for
27% of male ⎭ more than half of their sex partners.   188

6% of female ⎫ homosexuals prefer sexual partners to be
27% of male ⎭ masculine.   188

13% of female ⎫ homosexuals prefer sexual partners to be
1% of male ⎭ feminine.   188

46% of female ⎫ homosexuals who have been married say
46% of male ⎬ that their homosexuality had nothing to
         ⎭ do with the end of their marriages.   188

4

Work and Money

Females and Males Go to Work

99% of secretaries are female. 1% are male. [101]

96% of household cleaners and servants are female. 4% are male. [101]

95% of registered nurses are female. 5% are male. [101]

86% of librarians are female. 14% are male. [101]

83% of cashiers are female. 17% are male. [101]

66% of social workers are female. 34% are male. [101]

50% of bartenders are female. 50% are male. [101]

50% of cooks are female. 50% are male. [101]

22% of farmworkers are female. 78% are male. [101]

18% of barbers are female. 82% are male. [101]

15% of doctors are female. 85% are male. [101]
31% of new doctors are female. 69% are male. [101]

11% of police and detectives are female. 89% are male. [101]

9% of fishers, hunters, and trappers are female. 91% are male. [101]

9% of dentists are female. 91% are male. [101]
23% of new dentists are female. 77% are male. [101]

7% of engineers are female. 93% are male.   101

13% of new engineers are female. 87% are male.   101

4% of truck drivers are female. 96% are male.   101

2% of firefighters are female. 98% are male.   101

Females and Males and the Labor Force

54 millions females
66 million males } are in the work force.   101

45% of the labor force is female. 55% is male.   101

In 1890 17% of the labor force was female. 83% was male.
201

44% of females } age 16 and over are not in the labor
24% of males } force.   101

68% of employed females }
86% of employed males } work full time.   181

49% of employed females } work full time year round.
67% of employed males } 181

13% of disabled females }
23% of disabled males } work full time.   141

3.1 million females
4.1 million males } **work two or more jobs.**   193

Females and Males and Bosses

In the 1989 Fortune 500 there were 3 female CEOs and 497 male CEOs. 132

2% of the senior executives at 1989 Fortune 500 companies were female. 98% were male. 132

11% of franchises are owned by females. 89% are owned by males. 132

22% of the owners of small businesses are female. 77% are male. 107

3 million women
6.6 million men } are self-employed. 101

Females and Males and Their Jobs

47% of females
54% of males } consider their work more of a career than just a job. 199

31% of females
35% of males } are extremely satisfied with their chosen fields of work. 283

52% of females
33% of males } have worked less than 5 years at the jobs they held the longest. 118

8% of females
21% of males } have worked at least 20 years at the jobs they held the longest. 118

By the age of 64, women are away from their work an average of 14.7 years. Men are away an average of 1.6 years. 155

58% of females ⎱ expect to be employed by their current
63% of males ⎰ employers in five years. 199

43% of females ⎱ think they will eventually be promoted
50% of males ⎰ to a higher supervisory level. 200

16% of females ⎱ felt like quitting their jobs in the last
18% of males ⎰ month. 283

13% of females ⎱ would refuse to take a lie detector test
23% of males ⎰ even if it meant losing their jobs. 245

20% of females ⎱ went to work last weekend. 283
33% of males ⎰

20% of professional women ⎱ **who work full time work**
37% of professional men ⎰ **49 or more hours a week.**
326

22% of females ⎱ take a day off from work to indulge
28% of males ⎰ themselves.

Females and Males and Work

4% of women executives prefer a female boss. 29% of women executives prefer a male boss. 134

53% of females
38% of males } think that at work most men just don't take women seriously. 200

48% of females
63% of males } think that as more women rise to positions of authority in business it will not make the way business is done more gentle. 200

36% of females
42% of males } think the women's movement made things harder for males at work. 200

3% of female
21% of male } high school seniors do not think a woman should have exactly the same job opportunities as a man. 313

Females and Males and Who Should Work

39% of wives ⎱ believe that both they and their
31% of husbands ⎰ spouses should work. 233

75% of lesbians ⎱ believe that both they and their part-
77% of gay men ⎰ ners should work. 233

39% of female ⎱ high school seniors find unacceptable the
15% of male ⎰ thought of being in a marriage (without children) in which the husband works full time and the wife does not work. 313

77% of female ⎱ high school seniors find unacceptable the thought of being in a marriage (without
75% of male ⎰ children) in which the wife works full time and the husband does not work. 313

16% of wives ⎱ are predominantly centered on their work rather than on their relation-
34% of husbands ⎰ ships with their spouses. 233

16% of lesbians ⎱ are predominantly centered on their work rather than on their relationships
18% of gay men ⎰ with their lovers. 233

79% of wives who see their working husbands as successful are very satisfied with their marriages. 76% of husbands who see their working wives as successful are very satisfied with their marriages. 233

52% of wives who see their working husbands as unsuccessful are very satisfied with their marriages. 57% of husbands who see their working wives as unsuccessful are very satisfied with their marriages. 233

68% of females 27% of males } **would still want their spouses to work even if economics were not a factor.** 200

Females and Males and Job Security

Among employed people, if forced to choose:

26% of females 19% of males } would choose a job that pays quite a low income but that they were sure of keeping. 286

34% of females 33% of males } would choose a job that pays a good income, but that they have a fifty-fifty chance of losing. 286

34% of females 42% of males } would choose a job that pays an extremely high income if they make the grade, but that they are sure to lose if they don't. 286

Females and Males Get Paid

75% of all workers paid less than the minimum wage are female. 25% are male. 101

The median full-time earnings for females is $16,900. For males it is $26,000. 202

4% of females ⎱ age 15 and older earn at least $35,000 a
20% of males ⎰ year. 101

17% of females ⎱ age 15 and older earn less than $2,000 a
7% of males ⎰ year. 101

Females who went to college earn an average of $21,700 a
year. Males earn $36,000. 101

Females 65 years old or older earn an average of $13,800
a year. Males earn $27,200. 101

Corporate females at the level of vice-president or above
earn 58% of what males make. 157

For every dollar earned by male lawyers, female lawyers
earn 63 cents. 181

For every dollar earned by male computer
analysts, female computer analysts
earn 73 cents. 181

Females who had five or more
years of college earn an average of $28,600. Males earn
$46,300. 101

Female secretaries earn 33% less than male secretaries.
181

Female teachers earn 18% less than male teachers.   181

Wives age 15–24 earn, on average, 58% of husbands' earnings.   141

Wives' earnings are, on average, 45% of husbands' earnings.   141

The wife earns more than the husband in 18% of dual-earner marriages.   181

Females and Males Buy Things

Married females shop an average of 7.2 hours a week. Married males shop 4.9 hours a week.   148

Unmarried females shop an average of 6.3 hours a week. Unmarried males shop 4.3 hours a week.   148

Females with postdoctorate education shop an average of 8.4 hours a week. Males with postdoctorate education shop 3.8 hours a week.   148

38% of females}
32% of males } have bought something from the Sears, Penney, or Ward's catalog in the past year.   199

41% of females}
49% of males } have looked through the classifieds in the last month.   269

72% of females}
44% of males } consider shopping to be a pleasant experience.   312

Females and Males Don't Buy Things

57% of females}
54% of males } are not interested in owning a telephone answering machine.   282

91% of females}
88% of males } are not interested in owning a fax machine.   282

89% of females}
85% of males } **are not interested in owning a telephone in their car.**   282

64% of females}
58% of males } are not interested in owning a video camcorder.   282

85% of females}
79% of males } are not interested in owning a satellite TV dish.   282

Females and Males and Business

14% of females} have a highly favorable opinion of most
16% of males } large business corporations. 268

37% of females} have a highly favorable opinion of most
41% of males } small business companies. 268

3% of females} think the oil industry gives excellent value
3% of males } for the dollar. 268

33% of females} **would like to see less trade between
24% of males** } **the United States and foreign countries.** 271

48% of females} favor higher tariffs on imported goods.
47% of males } 281

20% of females} think Israel is one of the most important
20% of males } economic forces in world affairs today.
269

34% of females} think China is one of the most important
41% of males } economic forces in world affairs today.
269

48% of females} think Russia is one of the most important economic forces in world affairs
56% of males } today. 269

18% of females} think "consumer activist" has a negative
20% of males } connotation. 265

16% of females} think "Wall Street" has a negative connotation.
20% of males } notation. 265

Females and Males and Takeovers

8% of females }
15% of males   } would be bothered if an American company bought the company they work for. 182

70% of females }
70% of males   } would be bothered if a foreign company bought the company they work for. 182

26% of females }
39% of males   } think that if a foreign company buys an American one, the American company is likely to be more profitable. 182

23% of females }
34% of males   } think that if a foreign company buys an American one, the American company is likely to produce higher product quality. 182

5% of females }
6% of males   } think that if a foreign company buys an American one, it is likely that there will be higher wages. 182

43% of females }
55% of males   } think hostile corporate takeovers have done the economy of the country more harm than good. 238

30% of females }
37% of males   } think "corporate merger" has a negative connotation. 265

Females and Males and the Responsibilities of Business

38% of females⎫ think providing free medical insurance
40% of males ⎬ is a definite responsibility of business.
              285

22% of females⎫ think providing free life insurance is a
25% of males ⎬ definite responsibility of business. 285

89% of females⎫ favor guaranteed leave of absence for
85% of males ⎬ new working mothers. 173

64% of females⎫ favor guaranteed leave of absence for
50% of males ⎬ new working fathers. 173

52% of companies offer unpaid, job-protected leave to new mothers. 37% offer it to new fathers. 131

13% of females ⎱
12% of males ⎰ think providing or paying part of day-care costs for employed mothers is a definite responsibility of business. 285

27% of females ⎱
29% of males ⎰ think job training for the unemployed should be primarily the responsibility of business. 282

Females and Males Strike

The first reaction of 34% of females and 32% of males in a strike is to side with the union. 264

The first reaction of 23% of females and 27% of males in a strike is to side with the company. 264

61% of females ⎱
62% of males ⎰ think public school teachers should have the right to strike. 264

58% of females ⎱
58% of males ⎰ think postal workers should have the right to strike. 264

48% of females ⎱
43% of males ⎰ **think firemen should have the right to strike.** 264

47% of females ⎱
43% of males ⎰ **think policemen should have the right to strike.** 264

25% of females ⎱
23% of males ⎰ have stopped buying a product because of an organized boycott. 264

15% of female workers ⎱
23% of male workers ⎰ are represented by a labor union. 101

Females and Males and the Hard Sell

44% of females
45% of males
} think advertising can exert too much influence over what the media show or report. 271

**59% of females
51% of males
} do not like TV ads in which the competitors' products are named and compared with those of the advertiser.** 271

55% of females
41% of males
} pay attention to advertising in stores. 199

64% of females
55% of males
} pay attention to advertising on television. 199

63% of females ⎱ pay attention to advertising in news-
55% of males ⎰ papers. 199

41% of females ⎱ pay attention to advertising in the mail.
29% of males ⎰ 199

59% of females ⎱ think advertising keeps entertainment
64% of males ⎰ and news media from being government
financed and controlled. 271

Females and Males and Money

82% of females ⎱ often think about money. 182
80% of males ⎰

63% of females ⎱ often worry about money. 182
50% of males ⎰

55% of females ⎱ say their standard of living is comfort-
61% of males ⎰ able. 182

26% of females ⎱ think their chances of achieving the
30% of males ⎰ good life are very good. 282

5% of females ⎱ think their chances of achieving the
5% of males ⎰ good life are not good at all. 282

58% of females ⎱ **say the amount of money that their in-**
25% of males ⎰ **tended mate earns is important to**
them. 182

94% of females } would pick up a quarter they saw lying
95% of males   } in the street. 182

72% of females } would pick up a penny they saw lying in
73% of males   } the street. 182

82% of females } tend to feel that the rich get richer and
75% of males   } the poor get poorer. 241

The average net worth of single women is $62,800. The average net worth of single men is $83,900. The average net worth of married couples is $195,000. 145

The median net worth of single women is $18,400. The median net worth of single men is $24,200. The median net worth of married couples is $61,800. 145

13% of females ⎫ have no savings or investments. 182
9% of males ⎭

77% of females ⎫ own a credit card. 182
82% of males ⎭

33% of females ⎫ have charged $1,000 or more on credit
43% of males ⎭ cards in the last year. 182

11% of females ⎫ have deferred part of a credit card bill
12% of males ⎭ in the last month. 269

45% of females ⎫ **think the bad of credit cards out-**
45% of males ⎭ **weighs the good.** 270

74% of females ⎫ gave money to a charitable organization
80% of males ⎭ last year. 182

Females donate an average of $360 a year (1.4% of income) to charitable organizations. Males donate $590 a year (1.8% of income). 182

66% of wives ⎫ married 2–10 years favor pooling re-
74% of husbands ⎭ sources. 233

27% of female cohabitors ⎫ together 2–10 years favor
32% of male cohabitors ⎭ pooling resources. 233

40% of lesbians ⎫ together 2–10 years favor pooling re-
44% of gay men ⎭ sources. 233

Females and Males Invest

22% of females ⎱ feel quite competent in deciding
34% of males ⎰ how to invest money. 264

 5% of females ⎱ feel quite competent about making
10% of males ⎰ money in the stock market. 264

38% of females ⎱ feel totally at a loss about making
26% of males ⎰ money in the stock market. 264

3% of females ⎱ have bought stocks in the last month.
7% of males ⎰ 269

2% of females ⎱ have sold stocks in the last month.
4% of males ⎰ 269

50% of the country's stock shareowners are female.
50% are male. 133

Females and Males and the IRS

82% of females ⎱ filed federal income tax returns this
89% of males ⎰ year. 182

16% of females ⎱ think the IRS should not withhold tax
26% of males ⎰ refunds from people who are derelict in
paying alimony. 271

15% of females ⎱ think most people cheat on their income
17% of males ⎰ taxes. 283

35% of females ⎱ think tax reform has made the tax sys-
38% of males ⎰ tem less fair. 264

50% of females ⎱ have a favorable opinion of the IRS. 264
45% of males ⎰

5

School

Females and Males Teach School

2% of school superintendents are female. 98% are male. 227

12% of school principals are female. 88% are male. 227

47% of secondary school teachers are female. 53% are male. 227

83% of elementary school teachers are female. 17% are male. 227

98% of kindergarten teachers are female. 2% are male. 101

Females and Males Enroll in School

45% of females ⎫ age 5–19 were enrolled in school in
50% of males ⎭ 1850. 201

87% of females ⎫ age 5–19 were enrolled in school in
89% of males ⎭ 1970. 201

In 1940 the median number of years of school completed by females was 8.8. For males it was 8.6. 201

In 1970 the median number of years of school completed by females was 12.1. For males it was 12.2. 201

0.6% of females (564,000) ⎫ age 15 and over never went
0.6% of males (532,000) ⎭ to school. 142

75% of females ⎫ age 15 and over finished high school.
76% of males ⎭ 142

Females and Males and the Three Rs

64% of girls ⎱ in third grade say they're good with num-
66% of boys ⎰ bers. 169

48% of girls ⎱ in eleventh grade say they're good at math-
58% of boys ⎰ ematics. 169

64% of girls ⎱ in fourth grade say they like to write most
51% of boys ⎰ of the time. 169

51% of girls ⎱ in eleventh grade say they like to write most
28% of boys ⎰ of the time. 169

15% of females ⎱ think foreign languages should be given
17% of males ⎰ less attention in public schools. 268

19% of females ⎱ think sex education should be given less
17% of males ⎰ attention in public schools. 268

16% of females ⎱ think physical education should be given
15% of males ⎰ less attention in public schools. 268

Females and Males and School

44% of girls' parents ⎱ say school is one of their children's
28% of boys' parents ⎰ favorite activities.   178

 7% of females ⎱
14% of males   ⎰ age 8–17 do not like school.   244

37% of females ⎱ age 8–17 feel that boys feel more pres-
53% of males   ⎰ sures to do well in school than girls do.
244

42% of females ⎱ age 8–17 feel that girls feel more pres-
24% of males   ⎰ sures to do well in school than boys do.
244

In 9th and 10th grade math classes, teachers give 70% of encouraging remarks about academic ability and academic careers to male students. They give 90% of discouraging remarks about academic ability and academic careers to female students.   320

In elementary and junior high school classes, boys are 8 times more likely to call out for attention than girls.   196

32% of females | approve of spanking in public schools.
45% of males | 174

17% of females | think physical punishment is legally per-
25% of males | missible in their local schools.   302

67% of females | favor allowing prayers in public schools.
63% of males | 281

Females and Males Grade the Schools

29% of female | teenagers think students in their schools
35% of male | cannot read and write adequately.   244

15% of females | would grade the schools in their com-
16% of males | munities a D or F.   268

37% of females | think most teachers in their communi-
42% of males | ties expect too little from students.   268

48% of females | think discipline in local schools is not
50% of males | strict enough.   268

6% of females | think the school day should be length-
11% of males | ened by two hours and the school year
| by two months.   268

Females and Males Learn in a Different Tongue

9% of females
8% of males } think that in public schools with large Spanish-speaking enrollments there should be two sets of classes all the way through high school, one for English speakers, one for Spanish speakers. 268

36% of females
32% of males } think classes should be in Spanish for a year or two while Spanish-speaking children learn to speak English, and then classes in English from then on. 268

48% of females
52% of males } think classes should be only in English in public schools, with Spanish-speaking children required to learn English right from the start. 268

Female and Male Students and Their Parents

44% of poor black females
44% of poor black males } do not know the last grade their fathers completed in school. 298

29% of poor black females
49% of poor black males } do not know the last grade their mothers completed in school. 298

38% of females
42% of males } think most parents in their communities expect too little from students regarding school. 268

Female and Male Students Hear a Different Drummer

3,000 female \
7,000 male } 6-year-olds are in third grade.   143

55,000 female \
108,000 male } 15-year-olds are in eighth grade.   143

12,000 female \
5,000 male } **21-year-olds are in twelfth grade.**   143

18% of female \
10% of male } college students are age 35 or older.   149

Females and Males and Trouble at School

71% of female \
65% of male } teenage students say drinking goes on among peers in their school.   244

69% of female \
65% of male } teenage students say sexual activity goes on among peers in their school.   244

61% of female \
55% of male } teenage students say drug abuse goes on among peers in their school.   244

55% of female \
61% of male } teenage students say crime goes on among peers in their school.   244

52% of female \
34% of male } **teenage students say pregnancy goes on among peers in their school.**   244

85% of female ⎱ teenage students say smoking goes on
78% of male ⎰ among peers in their school. 244

Females and Males Teach College

10% of university presidents are female. 90% are male.
132

20% of college and university trustees are female. 80% are male. 132

37% of college and university teachers are female. 63% are male. 101

11% of tenured faculty members are female. 89% are male. 132

46% of female ⎱ college faculty members are tenured.
69% of male ⎰ 214

68% of female ⎱
55% of male ⎰ college presidents have Ph.Ds. 228

Less than 1% of coaches of intercollegiate men's teams are women. 52% of coaches of intercollegiate women's teams are men.   215

47% of female ⎱ college researchers rarely discuss their
38% of male ⎰ research with other faculty.   279

Females and Males Go to College

34% of females ⎱ age 25 and over finished at least one
41% of males ⎰ year of college.   142

17% of females ⎱ age 25 and over finished at least four
24% of males ⎰ years of college.   142

5% of females ⎱ age 25 and over finished at least five years
9% of males ⎰ of college.   142

12,000 females ⎱
22,000 males ⎰ receive doctoral degrees each year.   101

23 females ⎱
359 males ⎰ received doctoral degrees in 1900.   201

22,300 females ⎱
45,200 males ⎰ are awarded M.B.A.s each year.   274

38% of females ⎱ do not feel it is important that a person
42% of males ⎰ has a college education in order to be successful in the business world.   312

In the classrooms of coed colleges, female students speak 2½ times less often than male students.   195

Females and Males and School and Marriage

There are 2,729,000 families in which the husband has finished high school and the wife hasn't; 4,320,000 families in which the wife has finished high school and the husband hasn't. 170

There are 6,639,000 families in which the husband has finished four years of college and the wife hasn't; 2,509,000 families in which the wife has finished four years of college and the husband hasn't. 170

There are 6,639,000 families in which neither spouse has finished high school, and 6,039,000 in which both finished college. 170

Females and Males Are Tested

On the verbal part of the Scholastic Aptitude Test females average 425. Males average 435. 117

On the math part of the Scholastic Aptitude Test females average 453. Males average 500. 117

60% of students taking the Advanced Placement examination in English literature are female. 40% are male. 169

41% of students taking the Advanced Placement examination in math/calculus are female. 59% are male. 169

When they take the GRE (Graduate Record Examination):

80% of students declaring a graduate school major in education are female. 20% are male.   169

70% of students declaring in comparative literature are female. 30% are male.   169

65% declaring in anthropology are female. 35% are male. 169

50% declaring in biological sciences are female. 50% are male.   169

41% declaring in mathematics are female. 59% are male. 169

15% declaring in physics or engineering are female. 85% are male.   169

57% of females ⎫ age 13–17 have cheated on a test or
61% of males ⎭ exam.   325

81% of female ⎫ high school students think that if they
79% of male ⎭ cheated on a test, most of the students in
               the class would not care.   313

40% of females ⎫ think their children have never cheated
41% of males ⎭ in school.   302

6

Social and Political Issues

Females and Males Come to America

In 1820, 30% of immigrants to America were female. 70% were male. 201

In 1945, 65% of immigrants to America were female. 35% were male. 201

In 1970, 53% of immigrants to America were female. 47% were male. 201

For every 100 female legal immigrants there are 102 male legal immigrants. 293

For every 100 female illegal aliens there are 113 male illegal aliens. 293

For every 100 female refugees and asylees there are 130 male refugees and asylees. 293

52% of females
59% of males } think immigration laws should be changed to make immigration more difficult. 245

40% of females
53% of males } believe a person who entered the country illegally and remained for several years should be deported. 245

Females and Males and Private Clubs

30% of females
44% of males } think that private clubs should have the right to exclude prospective members on the basis of their sex.   119

14% of females
23% of males } think that private clubs should have the right to exclude prospective members on the basis of their race.   119

13% of females
21% of males } think that private clubs should have the right to exclude prospective members on the basis of their nationality.   119

12% of females
23% of males } think that private clubs should have the right to exclude prospective members on the basis of their religion.   119

Females and Males and Privilege

50% of females⎱ age 8–17 think boys have more privi-
50% of males ⎰ leges than girls. 244

30% of females⎱ age 8–17 think girls have more privi-
22% of males ⎰ leges than boys. 244

54% of females⎱ age 8–17 think that when males grow up
56% of males ⎰ they have more privileges than females.
244

23% of females⎱ age 8–17 think that when females grow
16% of males ⎰ up they have more privileges than
males. 244

49% of adult females⎱ **think there are more advantages**
51% of adult males ⎰ **in being a man than a woman.**
244

8% of adult females⎱ **think there are more advantages**
8% of adult males ⎰ **in being a woman than a man.**
244

Females and Males and Technology

40% of females⎱ favor more government spending on
53% of males ⎰ basic scientific research even if it means
raising taxes. 236

59% of females⎱ would like to see continued advances in
70% of males ⎰ exploration of space. 264

26% of females⎱ would like to see continued advances in
36% of males ⎰ advanced weaponry. 264

47% of females
55% of males $\Big\}$ would like to see continued advances in nuclear power for peaceful purposes. 264

33% of females
47% of males $\Big\}$ think the good of nuclear energy out-weighs the bad. 270

39% of females
32% of males $\Big\}$ think the bad of nuclear energy out-weighs the good. 270

17% of females
15% of males $\Big\}$ think that because of technology, life is worse today than it was fifty years ago. 282

14% of females
21% of males $\Big\}$ have used a computer in the last week. 263

34% of females
29% of males $\Big\}$ want no part of learning how to operate a computer. 265

3% of patents have been obtained by females and 97% by males. 297

5.5% of new patents are obtained by females and 94.5% by males. 297

3% of the members of the National Academy of Sciences are female. 97% are male. 216

30% of females⎱
38% of males ⎰ are particularly interested in scientific developments. 270

60% of females⎱
41% of males ⎰ are particularly interested in medical developments. 270

22% of females⎱
33% of males ⎰ think the new sophisticated games and toys are better for children than more traditional games and activities. 179

Females and Males and the Environment

48% of females⎱
42% of males ⎰ think that changes in the climate are a major problem. 171

45% of females⎱
40% of males ⎰ think land that will not produce enough food to feed people will be a very serious danger in the next five years. 171

11% of females⎱
18% of males ⎰ **would take a life with a higher standard of living but with health risks from the environment over a lower standard of living with much lower health risks.** 171

79% of females
74% of males } **would take a life with a lower standard of living with much lower health risks over a life with a higher standard of living but with health risks from the environment.** 171

22% of females
24% of males } think there are plants in the community that make products or use materials that cause them to worry about their safety or their neighbors' safety. 271

75% of females
64% of males } think having an atomic energy plant nearby would present dangers. 263

73% of females
71% of males } favor a mandatory 5-cent deposit on all beverage bottles and cans. 283

22% of females
20% of males } took empty cans or bottles to a recycling center in the last month. 269

47% of females
51% of males } favor a prohibition against plastic and styrofoam packaging at delis, fast-food restaurants, and other take-out food places. 283

8% of females
6% of males } think food scraps are causing severe consumer solid waste problems in their communities. 283

Females and Males and the Women's Movement

25% of females
15% of males } think women's organizations have done something to make their lives better. 200

3% of females
8% of males } think women's organizations have done something to make their lives worse. 200

60% of females
68% of males } think males' attitudes toward females have changed for the better in the past twenty years. 200

53% of females
48% of males } **think most of the males they know think they are better than females.** 200

29% of females
33% of males } think the women's movement is out of touch with the needs of most working females. 200

41% of females
57% of males } think males still run almost everything and usually don't include females when important decisions are made. 200

26% of females
19% of males } think females may have made some progress in the last twenty years, but now males are trying to take it away. 200

75% of females
68% of males } think that the women's movement has made romantic, social, and professional relationships between females and males more honest and open. 200

48% of females
33% of males
} think that although many females have better jobs and more opportunities than they did twenty years ago, they have had to give up too much in the process. 200

Females and Males and Race

77% of females
82% of males
} have friends of a different race. 177

55% of females
64% of males
} have had a guest of a different race in their homes. 177

23% of females
22% of males
} have been afraid of someone on account of his race. 177

16% of females
23% of males
} would like to see the federal government less active in ending discrimination against minorities. 165

73% of females
75% of males
} favor affirmative action programs in employment for blacks, provided there are no rigid quotas. 298

31% of females
31% of males
} favor school busing for racial integration. 281

51% of females
53% of males
} are opposed to school busing for racial integration. 281

90% of females
94% of males
} who have children who have been bused to go to school with children of other races think it worked out satisfactorily. 298

If they were the victim of a street crime, 31% of females and 34% of males think their attackers would most likely be white.   298

If they were the victims of a street crime, 31% of females and 37% of males think their attackers would most likely be black.   298

33% of females ⎱ think that blacks tend to have less am-
39% of males ⎰ bition than whites.   298

15% of females ⎱ **think blacks have less native intelli-**
19% of males ⎰ **gence than whites.**   298

19% of females ⎱
23% of males ⎰ think blacks breed crime.   298

Females and Males and the Homeless

33% of females ⎱ were approached by beggars last year.
44% of males ⎰ 182

61% of females ⎱ who were approached by beggars last
66% of males ⎰ year gave money.   182

Females who were approached by beggars last year gave money 22% of the times they were approached. Males gave money 28% of the times.   182

49% of females ⎱ **have given money to a homeless per-**
64% of males ⎰ **son.**   173

37% of females⎫
51% of males ⎬ think that if a homeless person tells a good story about his problems as part of an attempt to get a handout, the story is probably untrue. 173

11% of females⎫
17% of males ⎬ think most homeless people asking for handouts spend the money on drugs or alcohol. 173

22% of females⎫
33% of males ⎬ think people are homeless as a result of their own negligence or irresponsible behavior. 173

72% of females⎫
69% of males ⎬ favor more government spending for helping the homeless even if it means raising taxes. 236

27% of females⎫
20% of males ⎬ have thought of the possibility of becoming a homeless person. 182

13% of the homeless are single females. 49% are single males. 273

Females and Males and Animal Rights

85% of females⎫
75% of males ⎬ think animals have rights that limit humans. 172

65% of females⎫
51% of males ⎬ think the use of animals for cosmetic research should be prohibited by law. 172

55% of females⎫
35% of males ⎬ think killing animals to make leather from their skins should be prohibited by law. 172

68% of females } think killing animals to use their skins
58% of males } for fur coats should be prohibited by law. 172

20% of females } think training animals to perform for
12% of males } humans should be prohibited by law. 172

7% of females } think killing animals for food should be
4% of males } prohibited by law. 172

83% of females } have no desire to own a fur coat. 172
91% of males }

**24% of females } think hunting and killing animals for
50% of males } sport is acceptable.** 172

Females and Males Cast the Ballot

68% of females } were registered to vote in the 1988 pres-
65% of males } idential election. 144

58% of females } voted in the 1988 presidential election.
56% of males } 144

30% of females } are politically conservative. 182
39% of males }

12% of females } think "conservative" has a negative con-
14% of males } notation. 265

46% of females } are politically moderate. 182
45% of males }

14% of females⎫
12% of males ⎬ are politically liberal. 182

21% of females⎫ think "liberal" has a negative connota-
29% of males ⎬ tion. 265

27% of white and Asian females⎫ have voted for a black
35% of white and Asian males ⎬ candidate. 298

If their party nominated a qualified woman for president, 97% of females age 13–17 and 93% of males age
13–17 would vote for her. 325

If their party nominated a qualified black for president, 95% of females age 13–17 and 90% of males age
13–17 would vote for him. 325

If their party nominated a qualified Hispanic for president, 90% of females age 13–17 and 84% of males
age 13–17 would vote for him. 325

If their party nominated a qualified homosexual for
president, 50% of females age 13–17 and 37% of
males age 13–17 would vote for him. 325

Females and Males and Ruling the Country

**In the 101st Congress there are 98 male senators and 2
female senators; 410 male representatives and 25 female
representatives. 256**

34% of females⎫ think the American Constitution has
27% of males ⎬ served well, but it has not kept up with
the times and should be revised. 269

48% of females } think most politicians make promises
55% of males } they know they won't keep.   283

18% of females } think most people in government take
18% of males } payoffs in return for favors.   283

3% of females } daydream about being elected to politi-
5% of males } cal office.   271

30% of females } discussed politics with someone in the
41% of males } past week.   270

68% of female } state senators are married.   258
89% of male }

14% of female } state senators have a child under 12
28% of male } years old.   258

88% of female } state senators think their spouses' atti-
63% of male } tudes toward their political involvement
are very supportive.   258

46% of females
42% of males } tend to feel that the people running the country don't really care what happens. 241

56% of females
64% of males } have a favorable opinion of the CIA. 264

22% of females
19% of males } think the president of the United States is overpaid. 265

17% of females
28% of males } think the president of the United States is underpaid. 265

30% of females
35% of males } think most men are better suited emotionally for politics than most women are. 324

Females and Males and Government Money

**22% of females
19% of males } receive welfare benefits. 291**

14% of females
9% of males } over age 85 receive public assistance. 230

25% of females
26% of males } favor greatly decreased welfare programs. 281

64% of females
67% of males } favor more government spending on a child-care tax deduction for the poor even if it means raising taxes. 236

68% of female
52% of male } high school seniors would agree to a good plan to make a better life for the poor even if it cost them money. 313

Females and Males and the World

38% of females ⎱ take a good deal of interest in current
46% of males ⎰ events and world happenings. 263

36% of female ⎱ **high school seniors think nuclear or bi-**
25% of male ⎰ **ological annihilation will probably be**
the fate of all mankind, within their
lifetimes. 313

50% of females ⎱ think the U.S. should not sell arms and
35% of males ⎰ weapons to other countries. 283

47% of females ⎱
56% of males ⎰ rate Great Britain a close ally. 265

9% of females ⎱
20% of males ⎰ rate Japan a close ally. 265

9% of females ⎱
17% of males ⎰ rate West Germany a close ally. 265

36% of females ⎱ are very confident this nation will con-
45% of males ⎰ tinue to be a leader in world affairs. 284

Females and Males Defend the Country

8% of females ⎱ favor increasing the defense budget.
12% of males ⎰ 164

29% of females ⎱ favor maintaining the current spending
38% of males ⎰ level on SDI (Star Wars). 164

21% of females ⎱ favor maintaining the current spending
33% of males ⎰ level on the Stealth bomber. 164

Females and Males Go to War

Females make up 11% of the military. Males make up 89%. 275

11% of officers are female. 89% are male.   275

1.2% of brigadier generals are female. 98.8% are male. (All generals above brigadier are male.)   207

2% of colonels are female. 98% are male.   207

7% of majors are female. 93% are male.   207

14% of the Air Force is female. 86% is male.   275

11% of the Army is female. 89% is male.   275

10% of the Navy is female. 90% is male.   275

5% of the Marine Corps is female. 95% is male.   275

27% of females
 7% of males   } in the Army are divorced.   206

68% of people think young females have an obligation to their country to serve in the military during peacetime. 81% think young males have such an obligation.   290

83% of people think young females have an obligation to their country to serve in the military when the country is at war. 97% think young males have such an obligation.   290

22% of female
54% of male   } high school seniors think any military draft should include females as well as males.   313

56% of female ⎱ high school seniors would not volunteer
32% of male ⎰ for military service even if they felt that it was necessary for the U.S. to fight in a war. 313

83% of females ⎱ think there should be mandatory peri-
79% of males ⎰ odic drug testing of all members of the armed forces. 285

44% of females ⎱ in the Army are sexually harassed at
11% of males ⎰ work. 128

37% of female ⎱ high school seniors think servicemen
55% of male ⎰ should obey orders without question. 313

During the war in Vietnam the U.S. Army suffered 8 female casualties and 134,913 male casualties. 183

During World War II the U.S. armed forces suffered 361 female casualties and 1,075,884 male casualties. 183

Females and Males Send in the Troops

53% of females
66% of males } favor the use of American troops if an unfriendly government in Panama threatens to close the canal. 285

44% of females
61% of males } favor the use of American troops if Libya's Khaddafi renews his international terrorist activities. 285

42% of females
62% of males } favor the use of American troops if the Soviets invade western Europe. 285

25% of females
38% of males } favor the use of American troops if Philippine communists threaten to overthrow the Aquino government. 285

20% of females
30% of males } favor the use of American troops if Arabs invade Israel. 285

16% of females
34% of males } favor the use of American troops if North Korea invades South Korea. 285

Females and Males and Patriotism

77% of females ⎱
70% of males ⎰ think that in America today we need more patriotism. 176

65% of females ⎱
62% of males ⎰ think a person who buys only American-made products whenever possible is patriotic. 176

72% of females ⎱
70% of males ⎰ think someone who enlists in the Army is patriotic. 176

22% of females ⎱
20% of males ⎰ think an atheist is unpatriotic. 176

91% of females ⎱
95% of males ⎰ know Washington was the first president of the United States. 176

67% of females ⎱
63% of males ⎰ **know "The Star-Spangled Banner" is America's national anthem.** 176

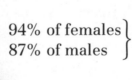

94% of females ⎱
87% of males ⎰ know the words to the Pledge of Allegiance to the American flag. 176

5% of females ⎱
6% of males ⎰ flew the American flag in the past week. 284

7

Knowledge and Beliefs

Females and Males Know Things and Don't Know Things

54% of females
71% of males } **think a bowel movement each day is necessary for good digestive health.** 114

14% of females
 8% of males } say they know a great deal about the gallbladder. 114

21% of females
15% of males } **would be troubled if astronomers discovered that the universe is expanding.** 116

37% of females
33% of males } who have some idea of what the Dow Jones Industrial Average means think it is the average price of Dow Jones stock on a given day. 264

60% of females
46% of males } have little or no idea of what is meant by bull market. 264

Young Females and Males Know Things

96% of females ⎫ age 13–17 know how to sew on a button.
80% of males ⎭ 325

76% of females ⎫ age 13–17 know how to bait a fishing
94% of males ⎭ hook. 325

74% of females ⎫ age 13–17 know how to play a musical
56% of males ⎭ instrument. 325

30% of females ⎫ age 13–17 know how to fix a leaking fau-
68% of males ⎭ cet. 325

Females and Males Believe Things

13% of females ⎫ think astrology can accurately predict
9% of males ⎭ the future. 173

16% of females ⎫ believe in UFOs. 286
20% of males ⎭

12% of females ⎫ believe in reincarnation. 286
10% of males ⎭

78% of females ⎫ **believe in heaven and hell.** 286
68% of males ⎭

34% of females
32% of males } think there are spirits or ghosts in the world that make their presence known to living people. 173

46% of females
40% of males } believe in ESP. 286

32% of females
41% of males } believe in the existence of life somewhere else in the universe. 286

33% of females
20% of males } **have had their fortune told by a fortune teller, palm reader, or psychic.**
173

33% of females
22% of males } read their horoscopes regularly. 173

5% of females
5% of males } believe in the special power of crystals. 286

Young Females and Males Believe Things

74% of females
73% of males } age 13–17 believe in angels.   325

58% of females
48% of males } age 13–17 believe in astrology.   111

11% of females
20% of males } age 13–17 believe in Bigfoot.   111

 9% of females
17% of males } age 13–17 believe in the Loch Ness monster.   111

18% of females
22% of males } age 8–12 believe alien spaceships have visited earth.   163

Females and Males Take Advice

44% of females
29% of males } follow Dear Abby.   166

43% of females
30% of males } follow Ann Landers.   166

22% of females
11% of males } follow Ask Dr. Brothers.   166

21% of females
10% of males } follow Miss Manners.   166

63% of females
43% of males } follow at least one advice columnist.   166

Females and Males and Risk

10% of females } think eating red meat is a high risk to
 8% of males   } people's health and safety.   284

16% of females } think eating food with preservatives is a
13% of males } high risk to people's health and safety.
284

23% of females } think flying in a plane is a high risk to
17% of males } people's health and safety.   284

29% of females } think living in an earthquake area is a
22% of males } high risk to people's health and safety.
284

40% of females } think eating food sprayed with pesti-
32% of males } cides is a high risk to people's health
            and safety.   284

42% of females ⎱ think drinking alcoholic beverages is a
31% of males ⎰ high risk to people's health and safety.
284

46% of females ⎱ think living where there is industrial air
41% of males ⎰ pollution is a high risk to people's health
and safety. 284

49% of females ⎱ think living near a chemical manufactur-
41% of males ⎰ ing plant is a high risk to people's health
and safety. 284

50% of females ⎱ think living near a nuclear power plant
37% of males ⎰ is a high risk to people's health and
safety. 284

65% of females ⎱ think smoking cigarettes is a high risk to
63% of males ⎰ people's health and safety. 284

29% of females ⎱ like to take chances. 312
35% of males ⎰

Females and Males Go to Church

75% of females ⎱ are members of a church or synagogue.
63% of males ⎰ 119

46% of females ⎱ attended church or synagogue in the last
38% of males ⎰ week. 119

61% of females ⎱ think religion is very important in their
46% of males ⎰ lives. 119

34% of females ⎱ have hardly any confidence in the peo-
43% of males ⎰ ple running organized religion. 240

35% of females ⎫ think "religious fundamentalist" has a
42% of males ⎭ negative connotation. 265

17% of females ⎫ have watched a preacher on TV in the
13% of males ⎭ past week. 284

52% of females ⎫ think "television evangelist" has a neg-
63% of males ⎭ ative connotation. 265

40% of females ⎫ do not feel a person who is religious is
46% of males ⎭ more apt to be an honest person. 312

39% of females ⎫
26% of males ⎭ frequently pray. 286

 8% of females ⎫
20% of males ⎭ almost never pray. 286

7% of people imagine God more as a mother than a father. 67% of people imagine God more as a father than a mother. 290

8% of ordained ministers are female. 92% are male.   106

42% of female ⎱
37% of male   ⎰ high school seniors think that if we just leave things to God, they will turn out for the best.   313

Catholic Females and Males

40% of Catholic females⎱
37% of Catholic males   ⎰ have tried to encourage someone to believe in Jesus Christ or to accept him as their Savior.   124

24% of Catholic females⎱
17% of Catholic males   ⎰ would say they've been born again or had a born-again experience.   124

63% of Catholic females⎱
57% of Catholic males   ⎰ think it is wrong to exclude females from the clergy.   124

22% of Catholic females⎱
12% of Catholic males   ⎰ would like to see a greater acceptance of divorce in the Catholic church.   124

88% of Catholic females⎱
83% of Catholic males   ⎰ think that loyal members of a religion may disagree with some of its teachings and still be considered faithful.   124

Females and Males and Good and Bad

51% of females ⎫
45% of males ⎭ think there are absolute standards of right and wrong to live by. 176

61% of females ⎫
73% of males ⎭ have done something they regard as dishonest or unethical. 176

28% of female ⎫
19% of male ⎭ high school seniors sometimes think they are no good at all. 313

37% of females ⎫
41% of males ⎭ do not feel an honest person is a good person. 312

Females and Males Feel Good and Bad

Females cry an average of 5.3 times a month. Males cry an average of 1.4 times a month.   134

90% of females ⎱ **consider themselves happy people.**
90% of males ⎰ 312

67% of females ⎱ **tend to feel that what they think**
55% of males ⎰ **doesn't count very much anymore.**
241

54% of females ⎱ are better off than they were 10 years
63% of males ⎰ ago, all things considered.   263

17% of females ⎱ are worse off than they were 10 years
12% of males ⎰ ago, all things considered.   263

45% of females ⎱
45% of males ⎰ are very satisfied with their lives.   199

7% of females ⎱
5% of males ⎰ frequently feel nervous or ill at ease.   286

5% of females ⎱ frequently wish they had not done some-
6% of males ⎰ thing.   286

10% of females ⎱ frequently wish they were someplace
10% of males ⎰ else.   286

3% of females ⎱ frequently wish they were somebody else.
2% of males ⎰ 286

8

TV, Movies, and Books

Females and Males Turn on the Tube

Female teens watch an average of 21 hours 18 minutes of TV a week. Male teens watch 22 hours 36 minutes.   254

Females age 18–34 watch an average of 28 hours 53 minutes of TV a week. Males age 18–34 watch 25 hours 44 minutes.   254

Females age 35–54 watch an average of 32 hours 28 minutes of TV a week. Males age 35–54 watch 27 hours 1 minute.   254

Females age 55 and over watch an average of 41 hours 1 minute of TV a week. Males age 55 and over watch 37 hours 32 minutes.   254

22% of females ⎱ say they spend too much time watching
33% of males   ⎰ TV.   179

12% of females ⎱ say they spend not enough time watch-
 6% of males   ⎰ ing TV.   179

57% of females ⎱ **think most TV programs are not worth**
64% of males   ⎰ **watching.**   179

66% of females ⎱ consider a TV set a necessity.   282
65% of males   ⎰

27% of females ⎱ think family life in the household cen-
24% of males   ⎰ ters around the TV.   179

In households with a television remote control, females control the remote 34% of the time. Males control it 55% of the time. 146

76% of women ⎫ watch sports on TV in an average week.
91% of men ⎭ 161

44% of females ⎫ prefer watching a sports event at home
61% of males ⎭ on TV to going out to a sports event. 281

77% of females ⎫ **will stop watching a show if it's too**
51% of males ⎭ **sexy or violent.** 179

17% of females ⎫ think the effect of TV on children is pos-
21% of males ⎭ itive. 179

44% of females ⎫ think the effect of TV on children is neg-
35% of males ⎭ ative. 179

66% of females ⎫ will turn off the TV because they don't
61% of males ⎭ approve of a show their child is watching. 179

41% of females ⎫ usually turn the TV on first and then find
46% of males ⎭ something to watch. 269

48% of females ⎫ usually turn the TV on only if they want
42% of males ⎭ to watch a certain program. 269

40% of females ⎫ frequently have the TV on even when
37% of males ⎭ they're not watching. 269

22% of females ⎫ have been on television at least once in
27% of males ⎭ their lives. 181

Females and Males and What Should Be on the Tube

23% of females } think viewers should decide what should
40% of males } be on TV, that there should not be standards prohibiting some material. 172

52% of females } think explicit and graphic depictions of
35% of males } violence should not be allowed on TV.
172

80% of females } **think ridiculing religious beliefs**
64% of males } **should not be allowed on TV.** 172

72% of females } **think ridiculing traditional values,**
56% of males } **such as marriage or motherhood,**
should not be allowed on TV. 172

43% of females } think mild profanity, using words such
62% of males } as "hell" or "damn," should be acceptable on TV any time of day. 172

think it is a good thing for religious
33% of females } groups like the Moral Majority to pres-
29% of males } sure and boycott advertisers whose
shows they find objectionable. 269

Females and Males on Prime-Time TV

33% of the characters on prime-time TV are female. 67% are male. 218

43% of the characters in sitcoms are female. 57% are male. 220

25% of the characters in action-adventure programs are female. 75% are male. 220

66% of the females on prime-time shows are age 18–35. 52% of the males on prime-time shows are age 35 or older. 220

3% of the female ⎱ characters on prime-time shows have
12% of the male ⎰ gray hair. 220

35% of the female ⎱ characters on prime-time shows are
 7% of the male ⎰ blond. 220

19% of the female ⎱ characters on prime-time shows are
12% of the male ⎰ married. 220

The marital status of 31% of the female and 58% of the male characters on prime-time shows is undetermined. 220

Female characters on prime-time shows are 10 times more likely to be wearing provocative attire than males. 220

18% of all cartoon characters with an identifiable sex are female. 82% are male. 219

Females and Males and Television News

23% of news readers are female. 77% are male. 219

21% of reporters are female. 79% are male. 219

9% of experts are female. 91% are male. 219

30% of people interviewed on the street are female. 70% are male. 219

16% of eyewitnesses are female. 84% are male. 219

5% of weathercasters are female. 95% are male. 222

0.4% of sportscasters are female. 99.6% are male. 222

59% of females ⎱ watch TV for their main source of news.
54% of males ⎰ 179

Females and Males and TV Commercials

52% of females ⎱ **think television stations should not be**
37% of males ⎰ **allowed to advertise beer and wine.**
139

68% of females ⎱ think television stations should not be
61% of males ⎰ allowed to advertise cigarettes. 139

42% of females ⎱ **think television stations should not be**
24% of males ⎰ **allowed to advertise tampons.** 139

48% of females ⎱ think television stations should not be
29% of males ⎰ allowed to advertise feminine hygiene
spray. 139

42% of females ⎫
31% of males   ⎭ think televisions stations should not be allowed to advertise contraceptives. 139

 8% of females ⎫
16% of males ⎭ think television stations should be allowed to advertise X-rated movies. 139

20% of females ⎫
35% of males   ⎭ think television stations should be allowed to advertise erotic lingerie. 139

Females and Males and TV and Sex

31% of females ⎫
23% of males   ⎭ think scenes that suggest, but do not actually show, sexual activity between adults should not be allowed on TV. 172

68% of females ⎫
58% of males   ⎭ **think that watching television tends to encourage teenagers to be sexually active.** 139

34% of females ⎫
29% of males   ⎭ think contraception is too controversial to be mentioned in television programs. 139

Females and Males Record on Their VCRs

62% of females
55% of males } often record full-length movies. 263

30% of females } often record miniseries and specials.
20% of males } 263

18% of females
34% of males } often record sports events. 263

17% of females
20% of males } often record documentaries. 263

17% of females
13% of males } often record situation comedies. 263

13% of females } often record weekly nighttime serials.
7% of males } 263

11% of females
7% of males } often record talk shows. 263

27% of females } really like to watch children's movies
17% of males } and cartoons. 263

4% of females } really like to watch exercise and fitness
1% of males } videos. 263

3% of females } really like to watch X-rated movies. 263
10% of males }

65% of females
69% of males } own a VCR. 268

Females and Males and the Soaps

33% of females ⎱ really like to watch daytime soap op-
  7% of males ⎰ eras. 263

19% of females ⎱ often record daytime serials and soap
  8% of males ⎰ operas with their VCRs. 263

  9% of actresses ⎱ in daytime soap operas earn more than
22% of actors   ⎰ $200,000 a year. 261

19% of actresses ⎱ **in daytime soap operas feel uncom-**
10% of actors ⎰ **fortable when performing intimate**
                   scenes. 261

Females and Males in R-Rated Pay-TV Programs

In R-rated pay-TV programs women dress in provocative clothing or lingerie in 54% of scenes. Men dress in provocative clothing in 10% of scenes. 217

Female characters go from fully clothed to either partially or completely nude in twice as many scenes as males. 217

Females and Males and the Flicks

69% of women ⎱ don't like profanity in movies. 125/126
44% of men   ⎰

72% of women
42% of men } **don't like nudity in movies.** 125/126

77% of women
41% of men } don't like violence in movies. 125/126

53% of females
47% of males } rarely go to the movies. 126/126

68% of females
69% of males } prefer watching movies at home to going out to see them at a theater. 281

Young Females and Males and the Flicks

100% of females
99% of males } age 13–17 have seen *The Wizard of Oz.* 325

66% of females
59% of males } age 13–17 have seen *Gone With the Wind.* 325

45% of females
37% of males } age 13–17 have seen *Singin' in the Rain.* 325

27% of females
30% of males } age 13–17 have seen *Casablanca.* 325

6% of females
12% of males } age 13–17 have seen *Citizen Kane.* 325

Females and Males and Smut

51% of females } think theater showing of X-rated movies
34% of males   should be totally banned.   245

43% of females } think the sale or rental of X-rated video
29% of males   cassettes for home viewing should be to-
                tally banned.   245

50% of females } think standards in their community re-
41% of males   garding the sale of sexually explicit ma-
                terial should be stricter than they are
                now.   245

80% of females } think magazines that show sexual vio-
71% of males   lence should be totally banned.   245

61% of females } think that pornography leads people
45% of males   to commit rape.   245

17% of females } have seen an X-rated movie in the last
31% of males   year.   322

Females and Males in X-Rated Movies

In X-rated movies, for a general audience, available at local
videocassete stores:

The males are always portrayed in heterosexual acts. 57%
of the females are heterosexual, 35% are bisexual, and 8%
are homosexual.   253

The male is in command in 78% of scenes of sexual domi-
nance. The female is in command in 22%. In 37% of the
scenes in which the female is dominating, she is dominating other females.   253

In 68% of exploitation scenes a male exploits one or more
females. Females are the exploiters in 23% of exploitation
scenes. In 38% of those scenes females are exploiting other
females.   253

In 71% of bondage scenes females are bound. In 29%
males are.   253

95% of masturbators are female. 5% are male.   253

**69% of full-frame genital shots are of female genitals.
31% are of male genitals.**   253

58% of female characters are identified as clerical/secre-
tarial workers, students, or housewives. 62% of male characters are identified as professionals or businessmen.   253

21% of voyeurs are female. 79% are male.   253

Females and Males and the Press

29% of the bylines on the front page of *The Washington Post* are female. 71% are male.   221

14% of the bylines on the front page of *The New York Times* are female. 86% are male.   221

14% of the directing editorships of the nation's daily newspapers are female. 86% are male.   132

6% of females ⎫
7% of males ⎭ are very confident we can depend on what we are told by the press.   284

23% of females ⎫
24% of males ⎭ think "the press" has a negative connotation. 265

Females and Males Read

40% of females ⎫
31% of males ⎭ read a book last weekend.   269

Reading a book means a good time for 51% of females and 34% of males.   286

23% of females ⎫
17% of males ⎭ took a book out at a library in the past month.   283

31% of females ⎫
21% of males ⎭ bought a paperback book in the past month.   283

15% of females ⎫
14% of males ⎭ bought a hardcover book in the past month.   283

54% of females ⎤ read the newspaper almost every day.
57% of males ⎦ 312

10% of females ⎤ think the publishing industry is nice for
10% of males ⎦ our country to have, but it isn't very important. 265

Females and Males in Children's Books

In American children's books:

There are 2.3 males in the title for every female. 209

There are 2.9 male adult central characters for every female. 209

There are 2.4 male child central characters for every female. 209

There are 1.7 male human central characters for every female. 209

There are 4.3 male animal central characters for every female. 209

In books that won the Caldecott Medal (for excellence in children's books) ten boys are pictured for every girl. 195

9

Sports and Leisure

Females and Males Play Hard

68% of women ⎱ actively participate in sports or fitness
78% of men ⎰ activities. 161

18 million women ⎱ **participate in aerobic exercising.**
3.2 million men ⎰ 101

27% of women ⎱ have walked a mile or more in the past
32% of men ⎰ twenty-four hours. 285

10 million women ⎱
14 million men ⎰ run or jog. 101

8 million women ⎱
7 million men ⎰ participate in calisthenics. 101

14 million women ⎱
22 million men ⎰ participate in weight training. 101

26% of women ⎱ exercise strenuously three or more times
41% of men ⎰ a week. 140

46% of women ⎱ think they are in good or excellent phys-
58% of men ⎰ ical shape. 161

60% of families with a mother alone and 25% with a father
alone engage in exercise or physical activities together.
177

60% of mothers ⎱ often attend team sports their children
69% of fathers ⎰ are playing in. 177

45% of girls ⎱
37% of boys ⎰ age 8–12 would like most to be the smartest kid in school.   162

30% of girls ⎱
24% of boys ⎰ age 8–12 would like most to be the most popular kid in school.   162

25% of girls ⎱
39% of boys ⎰ age 8–12 would like most to be the best athlete in school.   162

Females and Males and Sports

56% of women ⎱
63% of men ⎰ are interested in baseball.   161

48% of women ⎱
73% of men ⎰ are interested in pro football.   161

29% of females ⎱
26% of males ⎰ follow tennis.   167

21% of females ⎱
21% of males ⎰ follow bowling.   167

20% of females ⎱
17% of males ⎰ follow horseracing.   167

46% of the spectators at the Indy 500 are female. 54% are male.   147

Females and Males and Biggest Sports Thrill

The biggest sports thrill for 37% of women and 32% of men would be to get the winning hit in the final game of the World Series. 161

The biggest sports thrill for 24% of women and 35% of men would be to throw the winning touchdown in the Super Bowl. 161

The biggest sports thrill for 15% of women and 8% of men would be to ride the winning horse in the Kentucky Derby. 161

The biggest sports thrill for 2% of women and 10% of men would be to win the heavyweight boxing championship. 161

24% of women
36% of men } bet on sports events in the last year. 161

60% of women
59% of men } think female journalists should not be allowed in male athletes' locker rooms.
161

62% of females
94% of males } age 8–12 have heard of Magic Johnson. 162

Females and Males Run and Jump

10-year-old females run the 50-yard dash in an average 8.9 seconds. 10-year-old males run it in 8.6 seconds. 117
17-year-old females run the 50-yard dash in an average 8.2 seconds. 17-year-old males run it in 6.7 seconds. 117

10-year-old females broad jump an average 54.2 inches. 10-year-old males jump 59.2 inches.   117

17-year-old females broad jump an average 64.4 inches. 17-year-old males jump 87.1 inches.   117

50% of females⎱ age 6–12 cannot run a mile in less than
30% of males ⎰ 10 minutes.   321

55% of females⎱
25% of males ⎰ **age 6–12 cannot do one pull-up.**   321

Women walk, on average, 256 feet per minute. Men walk 245 feet per minute.   134

Using the nondominant arm, a 10-year-old male can throw a softball as far as a female.   320
Using the dominant arm, a 10-year-old male can throw a softball twice as far as a female.   320

Females and Males Set World Records

A female has run 100 meters in 10.49 seconds. A male has run the distance in 9.92 seconds.   256

A female has run a mile in 4 minutes 15.71 seconds. A male has run it in 3 minutes 46.32 seconds.   256

A female has run a marathon in 2 hours 21 minutes 6 seconds. A male has run it in 2 hours 6 minutes 50 seconds.   256

A female has high-jumped 6 feet 10¼ inches. A male has high-jumped 8 feet.   256

A female has long-jumped 24 feet 8¼ inches. A male has long-jumped 29 feet 2½ inches.   256

A female has swum 100 meters in 54.73 seconds. A male has swum the distance in 48.42 seconds.   256

A female has swum the 100-meter butterfly in 57.93 seconds. A male has swum it in 52.84 seconds.   256

A female has swum the 100-meter backstroke in 1 minute 0.59 seconds. A male has swum it in 54.91 seconds.   256

A female has lifted 286 pounds overhead. A male has lifted 560 pounds overhead.   320

A female has lifted 529 pounds in a squat. A male has lifted 1,200 pounds in a squat.   320

Females and Males at Leisure

3 million women
17 million men } hunt or shoot.   101

18 million women
35 million men } **fish.**   101

8% of females
9% of males } have gone out dancing in the last week.   284

Going dancing means a good time for 40% of females and 31% of males.   286

4 million women
8 million men } throw darts.   101

36% of females
31% of males } went to a mall last weekend.   269

43% of female
52% of male } high school seniors get together with friends every day.   117

46% of wives
32% of husbands } feel private time is very important.   233

45% of female
40% of male } high school seniors spend at least one hour of leisure time alone every day.   117

20% of females
25% of males } enjoy leisure time more away from home than at home.   281

47% of females ⎱ enjoy leisure time more at home than
44% of males ⎰ away from home. 281

72% of females ⎱ believe in getting as much fun out of life
45% of males ⎰ as they can. 199

Females and Males Gamble

17% of females ⎱ played games like bingo sponsored by a
12% of males ⎰ church or charitable group in the last
year. 285

6% of females ⎱ bet on a horse race in the last year. 285
10% of males ⎰

2% of females ⎱ bet on a dog race in the last year. 285
4% of males ⎰

1% of females ⎱ bet on jai alai in the last year. 285
2% of males ⎰

11% of females ⎱ gambled at a casino in the last year. 285
13% of males ⎰

7% of females ⎱ played card games like poker or black-
17% of males ⎰ jack for money, not at a casino, last year.
285

3% of females ⎱ placed sports bets at work, in a betting
14% of males ⎰ parlor, or through a bookie last year.
285

Females and Males Win the Lottery

37% of females ⎫ played a state-run lottery in the past
47% of males   ⎬ year. 285

71% of females ⎫
92% of males   ⎬ have bought a lottery ticket. 184

If they won a million-dollar lottery:

83% of females ⎫
77% of males   ⎬ would donate some to charity. 199

66% of females ⎫ would take a long, long vacation.
64% of males   ⎬ 199

62% of females ⎫ would move to a different house.
65% of males   ⎬ 199

59% of females ⎫ would invest it in stocks or bonds.
59% of males   ⎬ 199

37% of females ⎫ would buy a really expensive car.
44% of males   ⎬ 199

33% of females ⎫
37% of males   ⎬ would quit their job. 199

32% of females ⎫
28% of males   ⎬ would put it all in a bank. 199

29% of females ⎫ would go into business for them-
39% of males   ⎬ selves. 199

Females and Males Play Games

In the past two months:

2% of females
8% of males } played chess. 281

4% of females
3% of males } played bridge. 281

4% of females
3% of males } played pinochle. 281

6% of females
8% of males } played checkers. 281

7% of females
14% of males } played poker. 281

8% of females
8% of males } played Monopoly. 281

10% of females
6% of males } played Scrabble. 281

11% of females
14% of males } played an electronic TV game. 281

12% of females
11% of males } played Trivial Pursuit. 281

12% of females
9% of males } played rummy. 281

42% of females
44% of males } did not play a game. 281

Females and Males and Cheap Thrills

64% of females ⎱ enjoy or look forward to checking the
53% of males ⎰ mail. 282

43% of females ⎱ enjoy or look forward to getting in the
51% of males ⎰ house once their day is over. 282

41% of females ⎱ enjoy or look forward to being by them-
30% of males ⎰ selves. 282

37% of females ⎱ enjoy or look forward to having the tele-
20% of males ⎰ phone ring. 282

36% of females ⎱ enjoy going to or looking around a greet-
7% of males ⎰ ing card store. 286

28% of females ⎱ enjoy going to or looking around a pet
18% of males ⎰ store. 286

22% of females ⎱ enjoy or look forward to having the
14% of males ⎰ doorbell ring. 282

8% of females ⎱ enjoy or look forward to leaving the
10% of males ⎰ house in the morning. 282

Females and Males and Friends

63% of females say conversations with other females are important. 43% of males say so of calls with other males. 187

14% of females never call a female just to talk. 40% of males never call a male.   187

60% of conversations between females and 27% of conversations between males are on personal or emotional topics.   181

50% of divorced females ⎫ say their marriages had inter-
22% of divorced males ⎭ fered with their friendships. 210

13% of female ⎱ high school seniors have taken part in a
20% of male ⎰ fight pitting a group of their friends against another group in the last year. 245

40% of females ⎱ had friends over last weekend.   269
37% of males ⎰

65% of females ⎫ prefer getting together with friends in
63% of males ⎭ their home to going out with friends to a restaurant, bar, or club.   281

Females and Males Place Calls

44% of females ⎱ made a long-distance call in the last
40% of males ⎰ week. 263

23% of females ⎫ placed 10 or more calls to friends or rel-
19% of males ⎭ atives over 100 miles away in the last month.   264

42% of females ⎱ received a personal long-distance call in
36% of males ⎰ the last week. 263

15% of females ⎱ used a public telephone in the past
24% of males ⎰ twenty-four hours. 264

Females and Males at Christmas

Christmas is the favorite time of year for 56% of females and 41% of males. 173

38% of females ⎱ feel more stressed than usual during the
29% of males ⎰ Christmas season. 173

During the Christmas season, 65% of females and 44% of males enjoy picking out, buying, and wrapping presents for others. 173

42% of females ⎱ have a problem eating too much during
30% of males ⎰ the Christmas season. 173

30% of females
42% of males } **do shopping on Christmas Eve.** 192

3% of females ⎫ do not enjoy receiving presents from oth-
8% of males ⎭ ers during the Christmas season. 173

80% of females ⎫ enjoy putting up Christmas decorations.
60% of males ⎭ 173

4% of females ⎫ have a problem drinking too much alco-
9% of males ⎭ hol during the Christmas season. 173

35% of females ⎫ give a Christmas gift to their next-door
24% of males ⎭ neighbors. 175

10% of females ⎫ **think that in general they give nicer**
17% of males ⎭ **Christmas gifts than they receive.** 175

77% of females ⎫ think the true meaning of Christmas has
71% of males ⎭ become lost. 175

Females and Males and Excitement

9% of females ⎫ describe their daily existence as very ex-
13% of males ⎭ citing. 190

61% of females ⎫ say moral or religious considerations are
51% of males ⎬ very important limiting factors to the
              ⎭ spice they put in their life. 190

25% of females ⎫
31% of males ⎬ describe their job as very exciting.   190

Female and Male Exciting Figures

3% of females ⎫
6% of males ⎬ think Jesus Christ was history's most exciting figure.   190

4% of females ⎫
1% of males ⎬ think Jacqueline Kennedy Onassis was history's most exciting figure.   190

5% of females ⎫
0.2% of males ⎬ think Cleopatra was history's most exciting figure.   190

Females and Males, If They Could

Assuming they had the abilities, and time and money were no object:

56% of females
69% of males } would love to try being transported back into a period in history of their choice. 190

41% of females
57% of males } would love to try being transported 100 years into the future. 190

40% of females
63% of males } would love to try riding a raft down the Colorado River. 190

39% of females
42% of males } would love to try arguing a case before the U.S. Supreme Court. 190

77% of females
74% of males } would love to try traveling around the world in 80 days. 190

37% of females
25% males } would love to try writing a novel.   190

35% of females
43% of males } would love to try representing the U.S. at a summit conference with world leaders.   190

34% of females
27% of males } would love to try singing a solo on the stage of the Grand Ole Opry.   190

31% of females
27% of males } would love to try cooking dinner for the restaurant critic of *The New York Times.*   190

31% of females
21% of males } would love to try modeling Calvin Klein jeans on television.   190

25% of females
47% of males } would love to try managing a major league baseball team for a week.   190

24% of females
23% of males } would love to try conducting the Chicago Symphony at Carnegie Hall.   190

22% of females
30% of males } would love to try hosting the "Johnny Carson Show."   190

21% of females
41% of males } would love to try racing a car in the Indianapolis 500.   190

20% of females
37% of males } would love to try parachuting out of a plane.   190

16% of females
28% of males } would love to try climbing Mount Everest.   190

5% of females
11% of males } would love to try making an Evil Knievel–type jump on a motorcycle.   190

Females and Males on the Go

30% of overseas visitors to America are adult females. 63% are adult males.   115

40% of Americans traveling overseas are adult females. 54% are adult males.   115

38% of females ⎫
46% of males ⎭ have taken a trip by air at least 100 miles long in the last 2 years.   242

19% of female ⎫
10% of male ⎭ **air travelers have considered postponing an airline flight because of concerns over safety.**   242

11% of female ⎫
10% of male ⎭ air travelers fly first class.   242

20% of female ⎫
15% of male ⎭ personal travelers have taken a trip on a cruise ship.   287

Female and Male Dream Vacations

Europe is the dream vacation destination of 36% of female travelers (and 47% of single female travelers) and 30% of male travelers (and 31% of single male travelers).   287

Hawaii is the dream vacation destination of 26% of female travelers and 22% of male travelers.   287

The South Pacific is the dream vacation destination of 14% of female travelers and 18% of male travelers. 287

Asia is the dream vacation destination of 7% of female travelers and 12% of male travelers.   287

42% of females ⎱ prefer to relax and do little on vacation.
34% of males ⎰ 176

19% of females ⎱ didn't take a vacation last year.   176
11% of males ⎰

Females and Males Step on the Gas

87% of females ⎱ consider an automobile a necessity.   282
89% of males ⎰

12% of females ⎱ usually drive a stationwagon.   180
 7% of males ⎰

47% of female ⎱ **high school seniors who have a driver's**
65% of male ⎰ **license own a car.**   313

10% of females ⎱ receive a traffic ticket each year.   181
20% of males ⎰

21% of female
41% of male } **high school seniors received a traffic ticket or warning for a moving violation in the last year.** 245

5% of females
9% of males } receive a parking ticket each year. 181

63% of females
56% of males } always wear a seat belt when they are in the front seat of a car. 246

23% of females
34% of males } **would drive seventy mph or faster in good daytime conditions.** 264

55% of females
45% of males } never exceed the speed limit when they drive. 246

44% of females
31% of males } age 10–15 worry a lot about getting hurt or killed in a car accident. 247

73% of females
64% of males } age 10–15 worry a lot about their parents getting hurt or killed in a car accident. 247

17% of girls
35% of boys } age 8–12 would like to own a Lamborghini more than any other car. 162

On an average day 16,000 cars are sold to females. 21,000 cars are sold to males. 296

35% of females
43% of males } **who get to work by car would continue to do so no matter what changes were made to public transporation.** 283

10

Bodies and Beauty

Females and Males Are Sized

At birth the average female weighs 7 pounds and is 19.75 inches long. The average male baby weighs 7 pounds 9 ounces and is 20 inches long.   181

The tallest recorded female stood 8 feet 1¾ inches. The tallest recorded male stood 8 feet 11 inches tall.   102

The heaviest recorded female weighed 880 pounds. The heaviest recorded male weighed approximately 1,400 pounds. 102

The average woman wears size 10–12 dress and skirt, size 7 hat, 34–36B bra, 7½B shoes, size 6 ring. 181

The average man wears a size 40 regular suit, size 15½, 33 shirt, pants with waist size 34, size 7½ hat, 9½C or D shoes, size 9 or 10 ring. 181

Females and Males and Organs

The average weight of a white woman's brain is 1,252 grams (2.76 pounds). The average weight of a white man's brain is 1,392 grams (3.07 pounds). 320

The average weight of a black woman's brain is 1,158 grams (2.55 pounds). The average weight of a black man's brain is 1,286 grams (2.83 pounds). 320

The heart of the average woman weighs two ounces less than that of the average man. 320

The average woman has ⅘ gallon of blood. The average man has 1½ gallons of blood. 320

The average woman has one million fewer red blood cells in each drop of blood than the average man. 320

During maximal work a woman's heart can deliver 1 liter of oxygen to the body for every 7.1 liters of blood. A man's heart can deliver the same oxygen in 5.9 liters of blood.
223

Women sweat 24% to 70% less than men.   320

Women have 10% less lung volume than men of the same size.   320

Females and Males and Their Choppers

16% of females⎫
13% of males ⎬ age 18–74 have no teeth.   257

39% of females⎫
33% of males ⎬ age 18–74 have twenty-one or more de-cayed, missing, or filled teeth.   257

42% of females ⎱ age 18–74 are missing seven or more
39% of males ⎰ teeth. 257

20% of females ⎱
22% of males ⎰ age 18–74 are not missing teeth. 257

Females and Males and Muscle

The average female's leg strength is 72% of a male's. 223

The average female's grip strength is 57% of a male's. 223

The average female can arm curl 52% as much weight as a male. 223

The average female can bench press 37% as much weight as a male. 223

At age 5 muscle tissue constitutes 40% to 42% of total body weight of both sexes. By the time females reach 13, muscle tissue constitutes 45% of their total body weight and then decreases somewhat. By the time males reach 17, muscle tissue constitutes 54% of their total body weight. 320

At age 16 the total muscle mass of females is 80% of the total muscle mass of males. 320

A female's natural strength remains at about the same level attained at age 12. A male's natural (untrained) strength increases from puberty until age 25 or 30. 320

Females and Males Don't Like Their Bodies

3% of females
15% of males
} are dissatisfied with the size of their sex organs. 224

7% of females
9% of males
} are dissatisfied with the appearance of their sex organs. 224

32% of females
28% of males
} are dissatisifed with their upper torso. 186

57% of females
50% of males
} are dissatisfied with their mid-torso. 186

**50% of females
21% of males
}** **are dissatisfied with their lower torso.** 186

45% of females
32% of males
} don't like their overall body tone. 181

17% of females
20% of males
} are dissatisfied with their height. 186

31% of females
20% of males
} frequently think about their appearance. 286

Females and Males Fat and Skinny

Women's bodies average 27% fat. Men's bodies average 15% fat.   223

The lower limit of body fat for women is 12%. For men it is 3%.   223

White females age 18–74 weigh, on average, 143 pounds. White males weigh 173 pounds.   159

Black females age 18–74 weigh, on average, 157 pounds. Black males weigh 171 pounds.   159

26% of females
23% of males $\}$ are 10% to 20% overweight.   181

26% of females
12% of males $\}$ **are more than 20% overweight, that is, obese.**   181

24% of females
22% of males $\}$ are within their recommended weight range.   140

Females and Males Report Their Dimensions

Women report themselves, on average, 0.23 inches taller and 2.28 pounds lighter than they are. Men report themselves 0.57 inches taller and 0.91 pounds heavier than they are.   159

On average women overestimate their overall body measurements by 25%. Men overestimate by 13%.   186

6% of females ⎫ of normal weight think they are under-
16% of males ⎭ weight. 186

47% of females ⎫ of normal weight think they are over-
29% of males ⎭ weight. 186

100% of females ⎫ **who are overweight think they are**
90% of males ⎭ **overweight.** 186

41% of females ⎫
52% of males ⎭ think their weight is just right. 177

51% of females ⎫ describe their spouse's weight as just
58% of males ⎭ right. 177

49% of females ⎫ who judge themselves overweight like
55% of males ⎭ the way they look. 186

Females and Males Keep It Clean

Females age 18–24 spend 6.6 hours a week eating and 7.5 hours a week grooming. Males age 18–24 spend 7.2 hours a week eating and 5.3 hours a week grooming. 225

22% of females
18% of males } have brushed their teeth more than twice in the last twenty-four hours. 271

37% of females
18% of males } squeeze the toothpaste tube from the bottom. 311

30% of females
20% of males } have flossed their teeth in the last twenty-four hours. 271

43% of females
37% of males } have used mouthwash in the last twenty-four hours. 271

92% of females
86% of males } use deodorant. 134

47% of females
20% of males } lather up their hands with soap before they apply it to their body. 311

**15% of females
28% of males** } **never clean their belly button.** 311

31% of females
42% of males } clean their belly button every day. 311

**67% of females
67% of males** } **say their mate spends more time in the bathroom than they do.** 311

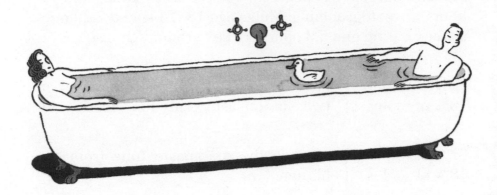

To indulge themselves, 46% of females and 20% of males, take a long bath.   270

Females and Males Look Beautiful

22% of females
68% of males } **like the way they look in the nude.**   311

28% of females consider themselves pretty. 42% of males consider themselves handsome.   181

16% of females daydream about being beautiful. 6% of males daydream about being handsome.   271

47% of females} consider themselves having average
33% of males } good looks.   181

73% of wives   } say their spouses are good-looking.
81% of husbands}   323

78% of females
87% of males } who remember themselves as being attractive teens rate their adult appearance favorably. 186

31% of wives
57% of husbands } feel it is important that their spouses are sexy-looking. 233

66% of female
34% of male } teenagers work on a tan. 120

45% of women
20% of men } say they wear uncomfortable shoes because they look good. 134

36% of female
29% of male } teenagers worry about losing their hair. 134

19% of females
19% of males } went to a barber or beauty shop in the last week. 284

**99% of females
94% of males** } **would change something about their personal appearance, if they could.** 267

24% of females
17% of males } think the cosmetics industry is very important or essential to our country. 265

Females and Males Get More Beautiful

165 females }
18 males } have face-lifts each day, on average. 129/130

169 females }
56 males } get nose jobs each day, on average. 129/130

If offered free of charge:

1% of females }
9% of males } would have hair transplants. 270

5% of females }
4% of males } would have nose remodeling. 270

9% of females }
10% of males } would use contact lenses. 270

10% of females }
4% of males } would have stomach stapling. 270

13% of females }
3% of males } would have face-lifts. 270

15% of females }
16% of males } would have teeth straightening. 270

39% of females }
49% of males } would have nothing done. 270

Females and Males Rate Their Own Beauty

On a scale of 1 to 10:

1% of females
1% of males
rate themselves a 1. 270

1% of females
1% of males
rate themselves a 2. 270

4% of females
3% of males
rate themselves a 3. 270

5% of females
4% of males
rate themselves a 4. 270

23% of females
20% of males
rate themselves a 5. 270

14% of females
15% of males
rate themselves a 6. 270

16% of females
18% of males
rate themselves a 7. 270

15% of females
14% of males
rate themsleves an 8. 270

4% of females
3% of males
rate themselves a 9. 270

6% of females
7% of males
rate themselves a 10. 270

Females rate themselves, on average, 6.3. Males rate themselves 6.5. 270

Females and Males Get Dressed

Women buy an average of 52 articles of clothing per year. Men buy 33. 134

58% of females} have bought clothes for themselves in
44% of males } the last month. 269

America produces 87 million pairs of jeans for women and 206 million pairs for men each year. 101

26% of females} wear a shirt with an advertisement or
34% of males } promotion for something. 284

21% of females} wear a jacket with the name and symbol
32% of males } of a club or team they belong to. 284

18% of females} wear a shirt or jacket with their own
22% of males } name or initials. 284

65% of females} put the right foot into their trousers first.
49% of males } 311

78% of females} **wear colored underwear.** 311
24% of males }

46% of females} feel it is important to be well dressed at
36% of males } all times. 312

11

Food

Females and Males Take Time to Eat

Females age 18–24 spend 6.6 hours a week eating. Males age 18–24 spend 7.2 hours a week eating.   225

Females age 35–44 spend 7.8 hours a week eating. Males age 35–44 spend 7.7 hours a week eating.   225

Females age 55–64 spend 9.9 hours a week eating. Males age 55–64 spend 10.7 hours a week eating.   225

Females without children spend 8.2 hours a week eating. Males without children spend 8.3 hours a week eating.   225

Females with at least one child under age 5 spend 7.2 hours a week eating. Males with at least one child under age 5 spend 7.4 hours a week eating.   225

Employed females spend 7.1 hours a week eating. Employed males spend 7.8 hours a week eating.   225

Unemployed females spend 9.2 hours a week eating. Unemployed males spend 9.8 hours a week eating.   225

Females and Males and How Often They Eat

34% of females
40% of males } eat 2 meals a day.   177

53% of females
48% of males } eat 3 meals a day.   177

  4% of females
10% of males } age 19–50 eat something 8 or more times a day.   309/310

Families with a mother alone eat dinner together 6.3 times a week. Families with father alone eat dinner together 3.7 times a week.   177

Females and Males Eat Sweets

50% of females
62% of males } eat candy at least once a week.   105

48% of females
17% of males } often feel guilty after eating candy.   105

70% of females
58% of males } have tried to reduce the amount of sugar in their diets.   177

12% of females
12% of males } chewed regular gum in the last 24 hours.   271

17% of females
10% of males } chewed sugarless gum in the last 24 hours.   271

30% of females ⎫ eat a special dessert, to indulge them-
17% of males ⎭ selves. 270

Females and Males Watch What They Eat

69% of females ⎫ have tried to reduce the amount of
55% of males ⎭ cholesterol in their diets. 177

71% of females ⎫ have tried to reduce the amount of
61% of males ⎭ salt in their diets. 177

59% of females ⎫ have tried to reduce the amount of
47% of males ⎭ preservatives in their diets. 177

Females and Males and Nutrients

Females age 19–50 eat food supplying an average of 1,661 Calories a day. Males age 19–50 eat 2,560 Calories a day. 309/310

Females age 19–50 eat food supplying 82% of the RDA (recommended dietary allowance) of food energy (calories). Males age 19–50 get 94% of the RDA of food energy. 309/310

Females age 19–50 average 79% of the RDA of calcium. Males age 19–50 average 115%. 309/310

Females age 19–50 average 144% of the RDA of protein. Males age 19–50 average 175%. 309/310

Females age 19–50 average 133% of the RDA of vitamin C. Males age 19–50 average 182%. 309/310

Females age 19–50 average 61% of the RDA of iron. Males age 19–50 average 159%. 309/310

36% of females ⎱ make a special effort to get enough iron.
17% of females ⎰ 268

55% of females ⎱ do not make a special effort to get
62% of males ⎰ enough of any vitamin. 268

Females and Males and Chow

12% of females
10% of males
} bought bottled water to drink as a substitute for tap water in the last week. 284

25% of females
16% of males
} **eat corn on the cob side to side, rather than in circles.** 311

18% of females
32% of males
} like their steak cooked rare. 311

34% of females
41% of males
} would like to see continued advances in synthetic foods. 264

7% of females
8% of males
} took a nonprescription antacid in the last 24 hours. 271

Females and Males and Hunger

9% of females
12% of males
} grades 3–12 go hungry daily because they simply don't get enough to eat. 266

32% of female
14% of male
} high school seniors often worry about hunger and poverty in our country. 313

77% of female
48% of male
} high school seniors would be willing to eat less meat and more grains and vegetables if it would help provide food for starving people. 313

45% of females
38% of males
} think the bad of food preservatives outweighs the good. 270

Females and Males Try to Slim

36% of females⎱ pay attention to the calories of every
16% of males ⎰ meal they eat.   103

44% of females⎱ **feel guilty eating foods they like.**   314
28% of males ⎰

51% of females⎱ grades 3–12 have been on a diet.   266
28% of males ⎰

65% of females⎱ begin at least one diet a year.   181
25% of males ⎰

60 million females⎱ **are on a diet, on an average day.**
41 million males ⎰ 296

33% of female ⎱ high school seniors have used diet pills.
 9% of male   ⎰ 198

                              have an eating disorder, such as
12% of teenage females⎱ anorexia nervosa, bulimia, or
 4% of teenage males ⎰ dieting to the point of starva-
                              tion. 181

95% of sufferers of anorexia are female. 5% are male. 138

Females and Males Pig Out

In a U.S. government study of 38,000 people ate over a
3-day period, the greatest recorded consumption:

**In a day a female consumed 31 cups of coffee. A male
consumed 64 cups.** 213

At a sitting a female consumed 24 tablespoons (68 pats) of butter. A male consumed 21 tablespoons (60 pats).   213

At a sitting a female consumed 35 pancakes. A male consumed 27 pancakes.   213

At a sitting a female consumed 1½ pizzas (12 inches in diameter). A male consumed 4 pizzas.   213

At a sitting a female consumed 16 tablespoons of peanut butter. A male consumed 28 tablespoons.   213

At a sitting a female consumed 2.1 pounds of beef. A male consumed 3.9 pounds.   213

At a sitting a female consumed 2 pounds of liver. A male consumed 1.1 pounds.   213

At a sitting a female consumed 43 teaspoons of sugar. A male consumed 88 teaspoons.   213

At a sitting a female consumed 19 slices of raw onion. A male consumed 18 slices.   213

Females and Males Eat Exotically

5% of females
11% of males
} have tried snake. 270

2% of females
5% of males
} really like snake. 270

16% of females
22% of males
} have tried brains. 270

6% of females
7% of males
} really like brains. 270

28% of females
38% of males
} have tried quail. 270

18% of females
27% of males
} really like quail. 270

30% of females
30% of males
} have tried caviar. 270

8% of females
8% of males
} really like caviar. 270

17% of females ⎫
23% of males ⎬ have tried snails.   270

8% of females ⎫
10% of males   ⎬ really like snails.   270

32% of females ⎫
37% of males   ⎬ have tried pig's feet.   270

17% of females ⎫
16% of males   ⎬ really like pig's feet.   270

9% of females ⎫
10% of males   ⎬ are very interested in gourmet foods.   284

Females and Males in the Kitchen

90% of females⎱ have gone food shopping in the last
69% of males ⎰ week. 263.

90% of married women⎱ say they do most of the cooking.
15% of married men ⎰ 104

14% of women⎱
25% of men ⎰ don't like to cook. 147

 7% of women⎱
35% of men ⎰ almost never cook. 147

On an average day females spend 51 minutes preparing meals. Males spend 15 minutes. 296

16% of females⎱ grades 3–12 say they usually prepare
11% of males ⎰ the meals at home. 266

77% of working mothers say they prepare dinner alone. 16% say the husband alone does. 2% says the oldest daughter does. 1% says the oldest son does. 229

64% of working mothers say they clean up after dinner alone. 17% say the husband alone does. 6% says the oldest daughter does. 5% says the oldest son does. 229

Females and Males Eat Out and Take Out

39% of females
46% of males } had dinner out in the last week. 284

55% of females
61% of males } had lunch out in the last week. 284

40% of females
41% of males } ate in a fast-food place last weekend. 269

47% of females
34% of males } do not eat at fast-food places. 177

1% of females
4% of males } eat at fast-food places seven or more times a week. 177

31% of families with a mother alone and 5% of families with a father alone do not eat fast food. 177

40% of females
46% of males } have bought take-out food to eat at home in the last week. 263

Cost aside, 67% of females and 78% of males would rather eat most dinners at home than at a restaurant. 286

Cost aside, 31% of females and 19% of males would rather eat most dinners at a restaurant than at home. 286

**74% of females
47% of males** } **find topless waitresses objectionable.** 324

12

Health and Death

Females and Males See the Doc

Females make 756 million visits to the doctor each year. Males make 515 million visits. 101

Females average 6.2 doctor visits a year. Males average 4.5 visits. 101

81% of females ⎫
67% of males ⎭ visit a physician each year. 118

83% of females ⎫
70% of males ⎭ have a personal doctor. 121

6% of people who have a personal doctor have a female doctor. 94% have a male doctor. 121

11% of females ⎫
0.3% of males ⎭ who go to the doctor are given a breast exam. 101

15% of females ⎫ age 17 and older enter the hospital each
10% of males   ⎭ year. 118

11% of females ⎫
 8% of males   ⎬ have an operation each year. 181

Females make 256 million visits to the dentist each year.
Males make 210 million visits. 101

52% of females ⎫
48% of males   ⎬ visit a dentist each year. 118

16% of females ⎫ have had major dental work done in the
18% of males   ⎭ last year. 282

44% of females ⎫ took a prescription drug in the past
28% of males   ⎭ week. 270

56% of females ⎫ took a nonprescription drug in the past
47% of males   ⎭ week. 270

2% of females ⎫ had their blood tested for AIDS in the
5% of males   ⎭ past year. 282

In anatomy books used in major medical schools, 11%
of illustrations with an identifiable gender show females. 64% of illustrations show males. (The others
have equal representation or are gender neutral.) 259

Females and Males Get Sick

10.5% of Americans with AIDS are female. 89.5% are male. 101

5% of females⎱ personally knew someone with AIDS in
5% of males ⎰ the past year. 282

41% of female⎱ teenage students think students with
45% of male ⎰ AIDS should not be allowed in public
                schools. 244

3% of females⎱ suffer from frequent constipation.   101
1% of males ⎰

17% of females⎱ suffer from arthritis.   101
 9% of males ⎰

5% of females⎱ suffer from migraines.   101
2% of males ⎰

 7% of females⎱ suffer from hearing impairments.   101
10% of males ⎰

5% of females⎱ have varicose veins of the lower extremi-
1% of males ⎰ ties. 256

18% of females⎱ have allergies.   181
22% of males ⎰

3% of females⎱ have cataracts.   256
1% of males ⎰

53% of females⎱ age 65–74 have hypertension.   159
44% of males ⎰

If told after an examination that they were likely to get an incurable disease that genetic engineering might help them avoid, 52% of females and 63% of males would undergo the genetic change.   267

24% of females
29% of males } say their health is excellent.   168

6% of females
3% of males } say their health is poor.   168

65% of females
75% of males } have life insurance.   101

Females and Males Suffer Outrageous Fortune

For every 2 mentally retarded females there are 3 mentally retarded males.   138

For every autistic female there are 3–4 autistic males.   138

For every hyperactive female child there are 6–9 hyperactive male children.   138

3% of females
7% of males } are bed-wetters at age 5.   138

For every female stutterer there are 3 male stutterers.   138

For every male who has suffered from a major depression, 2 females have.   138

For every male who has multiple personalities 3–9 females have them.   138

Male pedophiles are twice as likely to continue committing their acts if they desire boys rather than girls.   138

For every 100 males admitted to mental hospitals for neurosis, 168 females are admitted.   301

For every 100 males admitted to mental hospitals for functional psychosis, 127 females are admitted.   301

Females and Males and Abortion

52% of females
55% of males
} favor a woman's right to have an abortion early in her pregnancy for whatever reason.   172

56% of females
62% of males
} think a pill that allows females to terminate unintended pregnancy in the first few weeks should be made available.   248

61% of females
73% of males
} think the federal government should be less active in keeping females from having abortions.   165

62% of females
55% of males
} think abortion is a morally unacceptable method of family planning.   172

67% of female
42% of male
} Democratic state legislators would extend full abortion rights to minors.   204

45% of female ⎱ Republican state legislators would ex-
25% of male ⎰ tend full abortion rights to minors.   204

84% of females ⎱ think a state candidate's position on
67% of males ⎰ abortion is important.   278

18% of female ⎱ teenagers would handle an unplanned
31% of male ⎰ pregnancy with an abortion.   113

76% of recent articles on abortion in *The New York Times* and *The Washington Post* written by females are pro-choice. 55% of articles written by males are pro-choice. 260

50% of females ⎱ **support a law that the husband or**
64% of males ⎰ **partner of a woman seeking an abortion must be notified.**   278

Females and Males Feel Pain

78% of females ⎱ have had a headache in the last year.
68% of males ⎰ 168

53% of females ⎱ have had muscle pain in the last year.
54% of males ⎰ 168

53% of females ⎱ have had joint pain in the last year.   168
49% of males ⎰

13% of females ⎱ frequently have aching feet.   286
 9% of males ⎰

12% of females⎫
 8% of males ⎭ frequently have a backache. 286

1% of females⎫ have consulted an acupuncturist for pain.
3% of males ⎭ 168

2% of females⎫ have consulted a spiritual counselor for
1% of males ⎭ pain. 168

80% of females⎫ have taken a nonprescription pain re-
63% of males ⎭ liever. 168

Females and Males Feel Stress

22% of females⎫ feel stress and tension at the end of the
16% of males ⎭ day almost every day. 270

38% of females⎫ think the amount of money they have to
33% of males ⎭ live on is a major cause of stress. 270

28% of females
26% of males
} think the amount of work they have to get done in a day is a major cause of stress. 270

22% of females
11% of males
} think their children are a major cause of stress. 270

10% of females
 7% of males
} think their spouses are a major cause of stress. 270

 9% of females
11% of males
} think their bosses are a major cause of stress. 270

Females and Males Get Blue

To feel better when they are sad or depressed:

58% of females
29% of males
} telephone a friend. 153

39% of females
33% of males
} get together with friends. 153

31% of females
27% of males
} listen to music. 153

30% of females
18% of males
} pray. 153

26% of females
16% of males
} eat. 153

31% of females
7% of males } clean house.   153

23% of females
4% of males } cry.   153

21% of females
10% of males } take a bath or shower.   153

20% of females
19% of males } go to sleep.   153

19% of females
7% of males } go shopping.   153

18% of females
5% of males } cook.   153

12% of females
23% of males } play a sport or work out.   153

7% of females
18% of males } drink an alcoholic beverage.   153

Female and Male Students Get Blue and Talk to People

When they feel unhappy:

51% of female students talk to their mothers; 61% of their parents think they talk to their mothers.

40% of male students talk to their mothers; 54% of their parents think they talk to their mothers. 255

22% of female students talk to their fathers; 12% of their parents think they talk to their fathers.

28% of male students talk to their fathers; 23% of their parents think they talk to their fathers. 255

35% of female students talk to a sibling; 4% of their parents think they talk to a sibling.

25% of male students talk to a sibling; 3% of their parents think they talk to a sibling. 255

74% of female students talk to their friends; 11% of their parents think they talk to their friends.

48% of male students talk to their friends. 4% of their parents think they talk to their friends. 255

20% of female students talk to nobody; 1% of their parents think they talk to nobody.

34% of male students talk to nobody. 8% of their parents think they talk to nobody. 255

Females and Males Are Looked After

1,004,000 females ⎫ live in homes for the aged and depen-
  422,000 males ⎭ dent. 101

18% of elderly disabled females ⎫ are cared for by their
54% of elderly disabled males ⎭ spouses. 292

37% of elderly disabled females ⎫ are cared for by their
20% of elderly disabled males ⎭ children. 292

Females and Males Give up the Ghost

In 1900 the death rate for white females was 16.3 per 1,000. For white males it was 17.7 per 1,000. 201

In 1970 the death rate for white females was 8.1 per 1,000. For white males it was 10.9 per 1,000. 201

In 1900 the death rate for females under 1 year old was 145.4 per 1,000. For males under 1 year old it was 179.1 per 1,000. 201

In 1970 the death rate for females under 1 year old was 18.6 per 1,000. For males under 1 year old it was 24.1 per 1,000. 201

In 1900 the death rate for females age 1–4 was 19.1 per 1,000. For males age 1–4 it was 20.5 per 1,000. 201

In 1970 the death rate for females age 1–4 was 0.8 per 1,000. For males age 1–4 it was 0.9 per 1,000. 201

48 females ⎱ **age 15–24 die for each 100,000 each year.**
141 males ⎰ 117

66 females ⎱ age 25–34 die for each 100,000 each year.
179 males ⎰ 117

566,000 children under 18 have had their mothers die. 1,634,000 children under 18 have lost their fathers. 28,000 have lost both.   101

Females and Males and Heart Attacks

The death rate from cardiovascular disease is 77% higher for men than women.   158

Women who have heart attacks are twice as likely as men to die within the first few weeks.   316

39% of females ⎱ die within a year after a heart at-
31% of males ⎰ tack.   316

Females and Males and Calamity

47% of those who die in falls each year are female (5,400). 53% are male (6,000).   256

38% of those who die in fires or from burns each year are female (1,900). 62% are male (3,000).   256

30% of pedestrians killed in motor vehicles accidents are female. 70% are male.   289

29% of those who die in motor vehicles accidents each year are female (14,000). 71% are male (34,000).   256

29% of those who die from liquid or solid poisons each year are female (1,400). 71% are male (3,300).   256

24% of those who die of poison gas each year are female (250). 76% are male (760).   256

17% of those who drown each year are female (1,000). 83% are male (4,700).   256

14% of those who die in firearms accidents each year are female (200). 86% are male (1,300).   256

Females and Males Cash in Their Chips

6,700 females⎫
24,200 males ⎬ commit suicide each year.   101

470 females⎫
1,570 males ⎬ committed suicide in 1900.   201

2,600 females⎫
15,500 males ⎬ kill themselves with guns each year.   101

2,500 females⎫ kill themselves with poison each year.
3,500 males ⎬ 101

850 females⎫ hang or strangle themselves each year.
3,800 males ⎬ 101

Suicide attempts and self-inflicted injuries occur twice as often among girls as boys.   280

Females and Males and the Right to Commit Suicide

46% of females⎫
55% of males ⎬ think people have a right to end their lives if they have an incurable disease.   324

12% of females⎫
13% of males ⎬ think people have a right to end their lives if they are tired of living and are ready to die.   324

6% of females⎫
8% of males ⎬ think people have a right to end their lives if they have dishonored their families.   324

5% of females⎫
6% of males ⎬ think people have a right to end their lives if they have gone bankrupt.   324.

13

This and That

Females and Males Dream

22% of females
23% of males
} would need to make less than $50,000 a year to live the life they've always dreamed of. 199

14% of females
15% of males
} would need to make at least $1,000,000 a year to live the life they've always dreamed of. 199

28% of females ⎱ **think the American Dream is very**
37% of males ⎰ **much alive.** 300

On a scale of 1 to 10, females feel their position on the road to the American Dream is on average 5.9. Males average 5.7. 300

On a scale of 1 to 10, females ultimately expect to reach, on average, a position of 8.2 on the road to the American Dream. Males also expect to reach 8.2. 300

Females and Males Daydream

51% of females ⎱
47% of males ⎰ daydream about being rich. 271

45% of females ⎱ daydream about traveling to places
42% of males ⎰ around the world. 271

35% of females ⎱
29% of males ⎰ daydream about being smarter. 271

26% of females ⎱ daydream about having a better job.
33% of males ⎰ 271

24% of females ⎱ daydream about having back someone
22% of males ⎰ who was important to them. 271

16% of females ⎱
16% of males ⎰ daydream about being famous. 271

16% of females ⎱ daydream about being a great artist,
16% of males ⎰ musician, or writer. 271

12% of females daydream about having a romance with a handsome star. 10% of males daydream about having a romance with a beautiful star. 271

10% of females ⎱ daydream about being involved with the
 8% of males ⎰ media, TV, or movies. 271

 9% of females ⎱ daydream about having great power and
13% of males ⎰ influence. 271

8% of females ⎱ daydream about getting even with some-
9% of males ⎰ one. 271

 5% of females ⎱ daydream about being a great athlete.
16% of males ⎰ 271

Females and Males and Their Favorite Colors

Blue is the favorite color of $\begin{cases} 38\% \text{ of females} \\ 53\% \text{ of males.} \quad \text{285} \end{cases}$

Brown is the favorite color of $\begin{cases} 1\% \text{ of females} \\ 6\% \text{ of males.} \quad \text{285} \end{cases}$

Gray is the favorite color of $\begin{cases} 1\% \text{ of females} \\ 3\% \text{ of males.} \quad \text{285} \end{cases}$

Green is the favorite color of $\begin{cases} 9\% \text{ of females} \\ 7\% \text{ of males} \quad \text{285} \end{cases}$

Pink is the favorite color of $\begin{cases} 10\% \text{ of females} \\ 1\% \text{ of males.} \quad \text{285} \end{cases}$

Black is the favorite color of $\begin{cases} 3\% \text{ of females} \\ 4\% \text{ of males.} \quad \text{285} \end{cases}$

Purple or lavender is the favorite color of $\begin{cases} 6\% \text{ of females} \\ 2\% \text{ of males.} \end{cases}$ 285

Red is the favorite color of $\begin{cases} 13\% \text{ of females} \\ 12\% \text{ of males.} \end{cases}$ 285

White is the favorite color of $\begin{cases} 2\% \text{ of females} \\ 1\% \text{ of males.} \end{cases}$ 285

Yellow is the favorite color of $\begin{cases} 5\% \text{ of females} \\ 1\% \text{ of males.} \end{cases}$ 285

Females and Males on the Farm

In the farm population there are 109 males per 100 females. In the nonfarm population there are 94 males per 100 females. 151

$\left.\begin{array}{l} 8.3\% \text{ of females} \\ 6.4\% \text{ of males} \end{array}\right\}$ 15 and over are divorced.

$\left.\begin{array}{l} 1.6\% \text{ of females} \\ 4.7\% \text{ of males} \end{array}\right\}$ who live on farms are divorced. 151

$\left.\begin{array}{l} 28\% \text{ of females} \\ 4.3\% \text{ of males} \end{array}\right\}$ who live and work on farms are unpaid family workers. 151

Females and Males and Flowers and Vegetables

Females visit florists on average 2.8 times a year. Males average 3.8 visits.   108

49% of females⎱ have bought a floral arrangement for a
38% of males ⎰ funeral in the last year.   108

26% of females⎱ planted flowers outdoors in the last
22% of males ⎰ month.   269

11% of females⎱ planted vegetables in the last month.
13% of males ⎰ 269

23% of females ⎱ bought a houseplant in the last month.
14% of males ⎰ 269

17% of females ⎱
22% of males ⎰ bought fertilizer in the last month. 269

39% of females ⎱ are particularly interested in plants and
22% of males ⎰ gardening. 270

Females and Males Turn In

5% of females ⎱ age 30–35 snore. 181
20% of males ⎰

40% of females ⎱ age 60 and over snore. 181
60% of males ⎰

71% of females ⎱ say they dream while they sleep. 181
65% of males ⎰

4% of females ⎱ had a nightmare in the past 24 hours. 264
2% of males ⎰

10% of females ⎱ had a pleasant dream in the past 24
10% of males ⎰ hours. 264

5% of females ⎱ had insomnia in the past 24 hours. 264
3% of males ⎰

9% of females ⎱ overslept in the past 24 hours. 271
11% of males ⎰

26% of females ⎫
29% of males ⎬ took a nap in the past 24 hours. 271

53% of females ⎱ enjoy or look forward to going to sleep
51% of males ⎰ at night. 282

34% of females ⎱ enjoy or look forward to getting up in
31% of males ⎰ the morning. 282

34% of females ⎱ stayed up past midnight in the past 24
41% of males ⎰ hours. 271

27% of females ⎱ got up before 6:00 A.M. in the past 24
30% of males ⎰ hours. 271

Employed females sleep 55 hours a week. Employed males sleep 54 hours a week. 225

Unemployed females sleep 57 hours a week. Unemployed males sleep 60 hours a week. 225

Females and Males and Nighties

6% of females ⎫
19% of males ⎬ sleep in the nude. 181

19% of females ⎫
37% of males ⎬ sleep in pajamas. 181

4% of females ⎫
33% of males ⎬ sleep in underwear. 181

1% of females
2% of males } sleep in long johns.   181

Females and Males and Everything Else

31% of females
40% of males } think "yuppie" has a negative connotation.   265

45% of females
38% of males } did unpaid volunteer work in the past year.   276

12% of females
11% of males } celebrated something special in the past 24 hours.   264

35% of females
17% of males } stayed indoors for an entire day in the past week.   284

49% of females
60% of males } **think their greatest achievements are still ahead of them.**   312

66% of female
50% of male } high school seniors think finding purpose and meaning in their life is extremely important to them.   313

Getting older bothers 21% of females and 18% of males a lot.   199

34% of females
18% of males } are particularly interested in the lives of people in the entertainment world.   270

The record for nonstop talking for a female is 110½ hours. For a male it is 240 hours.   102

There are { 2,947,000 Girl Scouts
5,347,000 Boy Scouts.   101

5% of females
15% of males } always print when they write by hand.   135/136

33% of females
20% of males } have written a personal letter in the past week.   284

36% of females
40% of males } throw away mail trying to sell things without opening it.   269

15% of females
19% of males } have moved their place of residence in the past year.   282

35% of females
42% of males } age 13–17 would like to live in their home towns for the rest of their lives.   325

13% of females
17% of males } approve of surrogate motherhood under any circumstances.   178

34% of females ⎱ oppose surrogate motherhood regard-
30% of males ⎰ less of circumstances. 178

13% of females ⎱ **frequently talk to themselves.** 286
  8% of males ⎰

20% of females ⎱ frequently sing, hum, and whistle. 286
18% of males ⎰

 7% of females ⎱ frequently swear. 286
16% of males ⎰

15% of females ⎱ frequently feel tired. 286
12% of males ⎰

15% of females ⎱ frequently put off doing something they
12% of males ⎰ should do. 286

17% of females ⎱ had a craving in the past 24 hours. 271
12% of males ⎰

13% of females ⎱ make a special effort to get enough
 5% of males ⎰ fluoride. 268

5% of females ⎱ make a special effort to get enough phos-
5% of males ⎰ phates. 268

Appendix

101. *Statistical Abstract of the United States: 1989.* Bureau of the Census.
102. *1989 Guinness Book of World Records.* Bantam Books.
103. *The New York Times.* January 6, 1988.
104. *The New York Times.* February 24, 1988.
105. *News from the National Confectioners Association.*
106. *USA Today.* February 14, 1990.
107. *Business Week.* February 8, 1988.
108. *Society of American Florists Floral Marketing Report.* 1985.
109. *A Profile of Older Americans: 1987.* American Association of Retired Persons.
110. *USA Today.* February 23, 1988.
111. *The Gallup Youth Poll.* October 29, 1986.
112. *Handbook of Family Violence.* Edited by Vincent Van Hasselt, Randall Morrison, Alan Bellack, Michel Hersen. Plenum Press. 1988.
113. *Seventeen* magazine. February 1987.
114. *A National Survey of Public Perceptions of Digestive Health and Disease: Lack of Knowledge, Misinformation and Myth.* National Digestive Disease Education Program. 1984.
115. *Travel Industry World Yearbook: The Big Picture—1987.* Somerset Waters. Child and Waters.
116. "Contemporary Cosmological Beliefs." Alan Lightman, Jon Miller, Bonnie Leadbeater. *Social Studies of Science.* 1987.
117. *Youth Indicators—1988: Trends in the Well-Being of American Youth.* Office of Educational Research and Improvement. U.S. Department of Education.
118. *Vital and Health Statistics: Health Characteristics by Occupation and Industry of Longest Employment.* National Center for Health Statistics. June 1989.
119. *The Gallup Poll: Public Opinion 1988.*
120. "News Release." American Academy of Dermatology. 1987.
121. *Rights and Responsibilities, Part II: The Changing Health Care. Consumer and Patient/Doctor Relationship.* The American Board of Family Practice. 1987.
122. *Probing Public Sentiment on Israel and American Jews.* 1987 Roper Poll. David Singer and Renae Cohen. The American Jewish Committee, Institute of Human Relations.
123. *The Gallup Poll.* April 1987.
124. *Los Angeles Times* Survey. September 1987.
125. *USA Today.* October 24, 1989.
126. *USA Today.* October 23, 1989.
127. *USA Today.* September 20, 1989.
128. *Sexual Harassment in the Federal Government: An Update.* A Report to the President and the Congress of the United States by the U.S. Merit Systems Protection Board. June 1988.

129. *USA Today.* September 14, 1989.
130. *USA Today.* September 13, 1989.
131. *Parental Leave Fact Sheet.* Catalyst. 1989.
132. *Working Women Fact Sheet.* Catalyst. 1989.
133. *Shareownership 1985.* New York Stock Exchange.
134. *The Harper's Index.* Lewis Lapham, Michael Pollan, Eric Etheridge. Henry Holt. 1987.
135. *USA Today.* November 21, 1989.
136. *USA Today.* November 20, 1989.
137. *Uniform Crime Reports: Crime in the United States—1988.* Federal Bureau of Investigation. U.S. Department of Justice.
138. *Diagnostic and Statistical Manual of Mental Disorders: DSM-III-R.* The American Psychiatric Association. 1987.
139. *Attitudes about Television, Sex, and Contraception.* Conducted for Planned Parenthood by Louis Harris and Associates. 1987.
140. *The Prevention Index '87: A Report Card on the Nation's Health.* A Project of *Prevention* Magazine.
141. *Census and You: Monthly News from the U.S. Bureau of the Census.* October 1989.
142. *Educational Attainment in the United States: March 1987 and 1986.* Current Population Reports. Population Characteristics. Bureau of the Census.
143. *School Enrollment—Social and Economic Characteristics of Students: October 1986.* Bureau of the Census.
144. *Voting and Registration in the Election of November 1988.* Current Population Reports. Population Characteristics. Bureau of the Census.
145. *American Demographics.* June 1989.
146. *American Demographics.* May 1989.
147. *American Demographics.* April 1989.
148. *American Demographics.* February 1989.
149. *American Demographics.* January 1989.
150. *Marital Status and Living Arrangements: March 1988.* Current Population Reports. Population Characteristics. Bureau of the Census.
151. *Rural and Rural Farm Population: 1988.* Current Population Reports. Population Characteristics. Bureau of the Census.
152. *Who's Helping Out?—Supporting Networks Among American Families.* Household Economic Studies. Current Population Reports. Bureau of the Census.
153. *The Public Pulse.* June 1989. The Roper Organization.
154. *The Public Pulse.* October 1989. The Roper Organization.
155. *Male-Female Differences in Work Experience, Occupation, and Earnings: 1984.* Current Population Reports. Bureau of the Census. 1987.

156. *Household and Family Characteristics: March 1988.* Current Population Reports. Bureau of the Census.
157. *Time* Magazine. December 4, 1989.
158. *Statistical Bulletin.* Metropolitan Life Insurance Company. January–March 1989.
159. *Statistical Bulletin.* Metropolitan Life Insurance Company. April–June 1989.
160. *Statistical Bulletin.* Metropolitan Life Insurance Company. July–September 1989.
161. *Sports Illustrated Sports Poll '86.* Lieberman Research.
162. *Sports Illustrated* for Kids Omnibus Study. Prepared by Child's Play. May 1989.
163. *Sports Illustrated* for Kids Omnibus Study. Prepared by Child's Play. October 1989.
164. *The Harris Poll.* August 23, 1989.
165. *The Harris Poll.* November 2, 1989.
166. *The Harris Poll.* March 14, 1988.
167. *The Harris Poll.* March 30, 1989.
168. *The Nuprin Pain Report.* Louis Harris and Associates. 1985.
169. *ETS Policy Notes.* Educational Testing Service. October 1989.
170. *Household and Family Characteristics: March 1987.* Current Population Reports. Bureau of the Census.
171. *Public and Leadership Attitudes to the Environment in Four Continents.* Conducted for the United States Environment Programme. Louis Harris and Associates. 1989.
172. *Survey of American Adults.* Kane, Parsons, and Associates. Submitted to *Parents* Magazine. October 1989.
173. *Survey of American Adults.* Kane, Parsons, and Associates. Submitted to *Parents* Magazine. May 1989.
174. *Survey of American Adults.* Kane, Parsons, and Associates. Submitted to *Parents* Magazine. October 1988.
175. *Survey of American Adults.* Kane, Parsons, and Associates. Submitted to *Parents* Magazine. June 1988.
176. *Survey of American Adults.* Kane, Parsons, and Associates. Submitted to *Parents* Magazine. February 1989.
177. *Survey of American Adults.* Kane, Parsons, and Associates. Submitted to *Parents* Magazine. November 1987.
178. *Survey of American Adults.* Kane, Parsons, and Associates. Submitted to *Parents* Magazine. June 1987.
179. *Survey of American Adults.* Kane, Parsons, and Associates. Submitted to *Parents* Magazine. January 1987.
180. *Survey of American Adults.* Kane, Parsons, and Associates. Submitted to *Parents* Magazine. October 1986.
181. *Almanac of the American People.* Tom and Nancy Biracree. Facts on File. 1988.

182. *Americans and Their Money. Money* Magazine. 1988.
183. U.S. Army Center of Military History.
184. *USA Today.* December 13, 1989.
185. *Psychology Today.* July 1987.
186. *Psychology Today.* April 1986.
187. *Psychology Today.* June 1984.
188. *Homosexualities: A Study of Diversity among Men and Women.* Alan Bell and Martin Weinberg. Simon and Schuster. 1978.
189. *Violence in Dating Relationships: Emerging Social Issues.* Edited by Maureen Pirog-Good and Jan Stets. Praeger Publishers. 1989.
190. *Popeye's Spice in Your Life Series.* Kane, Parsons, and Associates. Submitted to Popeye's Famous Fried Chicken. 1983.
191. *Journal of Marriage and the Family.* February 1985.
192. *USA Today.* December 20, 1989.
193. *USA Today.* December 14, 1989.
194. *USA Today.* December 6, 1989.
195. *Better Homes and Gardens.* February 1988.
196. "Is the OK Classroom OK?" David Sadker and Myra Sadker. *Phi Delta Kappan.* January 1985.
197. *National Household Survey on Drug Abuse: Population Estimates 1988.* National Institute on Drug Abuse. U.S. Department of Health and Human Services.
198. *Drug Use, Drinking, and Smoking: National Survey Results from High School, College, and Young Adult Populations 1975–1988.* National Institute on Drug Abuse. U.S. Department of Health and Human Services.
199. *The American Consumer.* R. H. Bruskin Associates Market Research. 1988.
200. *The New York Times* Poll. Women's Survey. June 20–25, 1989.
201. *Historical Statistics of the United States—Colonial Times to 1970.* Bureau of the Census.
202. *Hersay.* The Women's News Institute. February 6, 1989.
203. *Hersay.* The Women's News Institute. May 15, 1989.
204. *Hersay.* The Women's News Institute. June 12, 1989.
205. *The Family in America.* A Publication of the Rockford Institute Center on the Family in America. September 1989.
206. *The Family in America.* A Publication of the Rockford Institute Center on the Family in America. December 1989.
207. *Minerva.* Quarterly Report on Women and the Military. Summer 1989.
208. *Gender and Society.* December 1989.
209. *Gender and Society.* March 1989.
210. *Gender and Society.* September 1988.
211. *Family Planning Perspectives.* May/June 1988.

212. *Family Planning Perspectives.* November/December 1988.
213. *Foods Commonly Eaten by Individuals: Amount Per Day and Per Eating Occasion.* Human Nutrition Information Service. U.S. Department of Agriculture. 1982.
214. *On Campus with Women.* Spring 1989.
215. *On Campus with Women.* Winter 1989.
216. *On Campus with Women.* Summer 1988.
217. *Media Report to Women.* March/April 1986.
218. *Media Report to Women.* November/December 1986.
219. *Media Report to Women.* July/August 1987.
220. *Media Report to Women.* November/December 1987.
221. *Media Report to Women.* March/April 1988.
222. *Media Report to Women.* May/June 1988.
223. *Sex Differences in Human Performance.* Edited by Mary Anne Baker. John Wiley and Sons. 1987.
224. *Mirror, Mirror . . . The Importance of Looks in Everyday Life.* Elaine Hatfield and Susan Spracher. State University of New York Press. 1986.
225. *American Demographics.* November 1989.
226. *American Demographics.* July 1989.
227. *New Directions for Administrative Preparation.* Edited by F. C. Wendel and M. T. Bryant. University Council for Educational Administration Monograph Series. 1988.
228. *The American College President: A Contemporary Profile.* Madeleine Green. American Council on Education. April 1988.
229. *Working Mother.* February 1988.
230. *Society.* May/June 1988.
231. *Society.* July/August 1988.
232. *Society.* September/October 1989.
233. *American Couples.* Philip Blumstein and Pepper Schwartz. Pocket Books. 1985.
234. *The Harris Poll.* November 20, 1988.
235. *The Harris Poll.* November 24, 1988.
236. *The Harris Poll.* March 12, 1989.
237. *The Harris Poll.* April 9, 1989.
238. *The Harris Poll.* March 26, 1989.
239. *The Harris Poll.* May 14, 1989.
240. *The Harris Poll.* July 9, 1989.
241. *The Harris Poll.* October 29, 1989.
242. *Business Week/Harris Poll.* December 19, 1988.
243. *The Office Environment Index 1989.* Conducted for Steelcase. Louis Harris and Associates.
244. *The American Chicle Youth Poll.* Commissioned by the American Chicle Group, Warner-Lambert Company. Conducted by the Roper Organization. 1987.

245. *Sourcebook of Criminal Justice Statistics—1987.* U.S. Department of Justice.

246. *Auto Safety in America 1989.* A General Motors/*Prevention* Magazine report from research by Louis Harris and Associates.

247. *Kids and Seat Belts.* Conducted for the American Coalition for Traffic Safety. Louis Harris and Associates. 1988.

248. *Public Attitudes toward Teenage Pregnancy, Sex Education, and Birth Control.* Conducted for Planned Parenthood Federation of America. Louis Harris and Associates. 1988.

249. *American Teens Speak: Sex, Myths, TV, and Birth Control.* Conducted for Planned Parenthood Federation of America. Louis Harris and Associates. 1986.

250. *Public Attitudes about Sex Education, Family Planning, and Abortion in the United States.* Conducted for Planned Parenthood Federation of America. Louis Harris and Associates. 1985.

251. *The Lear's Report: A Self-Portrait of the Woman Who Wasn't Born Yesterday.* Louis Harris and Associates. 1988.

252. *Psychology of Women Quarterly.* December 1988.

253. *Psychology of Women Quarterly.* September 1988.

254. *The 1990 Information Please Almanac.* Houghton-Mifflin.

255. *Health: You've Got to Be Taught. An Evaluation of Comprehensive Health Education in American Public Schools.* Conducted for Metropolitan Life Foundation. Louis Harris and Associates. 1988.

256. *The World Almanac and Book of Facts: 1990.*

257. *Decayed, Missing, and Filled Teeth among Persons 1–74 Years.* National Center for Health Statistics. U.S. Department of Health and Human Services. 1981.

258. *Women and Politics.* Volume 9, Number 2. 1989.

259. *Psychology of Women Quarterly.* December 1986.

260. *Media Report to Women.* January/February 1990.

261. *Media Report to Women.* November/December 1989.

262. *Media Report to Women.* September/October 1989.

263. *Roper Reports.* December 1989.

264. *Roper Reports.* November 1989.

265. *Roper Reports.* October 1989.

266. *The Kellogg Children's Nutrition Survey.* Conducted for the Kellogg Company by Louis Harris and Associates. 1989.

267. *Inside America.* Louis Harris. Vintage. 1987.

268. *Roper Reports.* August 1989.

269. *Roper Reports.* July 1989.

270. *Roper Reports.* June 1989.

271. *Roper Reports.* May 1989.

272. *USA Today.* January 10, 1990.

273. *USA Today.* November 11, 1989.

274. *USA Today.* January 18, 1990.

275. *New York Newsday.* January 9, 1990.
276. *The New York Times* (National). November 24, 1989.
277. *USA Today.* November 17, 1989.
278. *USA Today.* January 2, 1990.
279. *USA Today.* December 11, 1989.
280. *USA Today.* December 7, 1989.
281. *Roper Reports.* April 1989.
282. *Roper Reports.* February 1989.
283. *Roper Reports.* January 1989.
284. *Roper Reports.* December 1988.
285. *Roper Reports.* November 1988.
286. *Roper Reports.* September 1988.
287. *The 1989 Travel and Leisure Study—A Survey of Traveling Americans.* Conducted for *Travel and Leisure* Magazine. Louis Harris and Associates.
288. *Success in America: The CIGNA Study of the Upper-Affluent.* Conducted for CIGNA Individual Financial Services Company. Louis Harris and Associates. 1987.
289. *National Center for Statistics and Analysis 1987 Fatality Facts.* October 1988. National Highway Traffic Safety Administration.
290. *General Social Surveys, 1972–1987.* Conducted for the National Data Program for the Social Sciences at National Opinion Research Center, University of Chicago.
291. *America's Welfare Population: Who Gets What?* William P. O'Hare. Population Reference Bureau. 1987
292. *Population Bulletin.* September 1988.
293. *Population Bulletin.* November 1986.
294. *USA Today.* February 1, 1990.
295. *USA Today.* January 24, 1990.
296. *On an Average Day.* Tom Heymann. Fawcett Columbine. 1989.
297. *The New York Times.* January 20, 1990.
298. *The Unfinished Agenda on Race in America.* Conducted by Louis Harris and Associates. 1989.
299. *Between Parents and Children: A USA Weekend/Roper Report on Consumer Decision Making in American Familes.* 1989.
300. *The American Dream.* Conducted for *The Wall Street Journal* by the Roper Organization. 1987.
301. *Gender and Disordered Behavior: Sex Differences in Psychopathology.* Edited by Edith S. Gomberg and Violet Franks. Brunner/Mazel. 1979.
302. *Attitudes toward Corporal Punishment in American Homes and Schools.* Commissioned by Rodale Press and conducted by Louis Harris and Associates. 1988.
303. *Temple University News Release.* Dr. Irwin Hyman, Director of the National Center for the Study of Corporal Punishment and Alternatives. 1989.

304. *Females, Males, and Sexuality.* Edited by Kathryn Kelley. State University of New York Press. 1987.
305. *Archives of Sexual Behavior.* February 1988.
306. *Archives of Sexual Behavior.* April 1988.
307. *Archives of Sexual Behavior.* December 1988.
308. *Archives of Sexual Behavior.* February 1987.
309. *Nationwide Food Consumption Survey—Continuing Survey of Food Intakes by Individuals. Women 19–50 Years and the Children, 1–5 Years. 1986.* Human Nutrition Information Service. U.S. Department of Agriculture.
310. *Nationwide Food Consumption Survey—Continuing Survey of Food Intakes by Individuals. Men 19–50 Years. 1985.* Human Nutrition Information Service. U.S. Department of Agriculture.
311. *The First Really Important Survey of American Habits.* Mel Poretz and Barry Sinrod. Price Stern Sloan. 1989.
312. *America in the Eighties.* R. H. Bruskin Associates Market Research. 1985.
313. *Monitoring the Future: Questionnaire Responses from the Nation's High School Seniors.* Jerald Bachman, Lloyd Johnston, Patrick O'Malley. Institute for Social Research, The University of Michigan. 1986.
314. *USA Today.* February 21, 1990.
315. *Perspective.* November 1989.
316. *The New York Times Magazine.* February 4, 1990.
317. *USA Today.* February 22, 1990.
318. *USA Today.* April 23, 1984.
319. *USA Today.* February 23, 1990.
320. *Men and Women in Biological Prespective.* Aman Khan, Joseph Cataio. Praeger Publishers. 1984.
321. *USA Today.* March 15, 1990.
322. *USA Today.* March 27, 1990.
323. *Good Housekeeping.* June 1990.
324. *Trends in Public Opinion: A Compendium of Survey Data.* Richard Niemi, John Mueller, Tom W. Smith. Greenwood Press. 1989.
325. *America's Youth 1977–1988.* The Gallup Organization, 1988.
326. *The New York Times.* June 3, 1990.